The
AGNELLI GARDENS
at VILLAR PEROSA

The AGNELLI GARDENS at VILLAR PEROSA

Two Centuries of a Family Retreat

By Marella Agnelli

Essay by Marella Agnelli and Marella Caracciolo
with commentaries by Paolo Pejrone

HARRY N. ABRAMS, INC., PUBLISHERS

Editor, English-language edition: *Ruth A. Peltason*
Design Coordinator, English-language edition: *Ana Rogers*
Translated from the Italian: *Alexandra Bonfante-Warren* and *Karin Ford*

Page 3: Cornus kousa chinensis. *Pages 6–7: A terrace at midday. Pages 8–9: A wooden gate separates the courtyard from the garden on the west side of the villa. Pages 10–13: A massing of spring flowers. Pages 14–15: A sculpture by Magritte framed by 'Iceberg' roses. Pages 16–17: The gardens and villa. Pages 18–19: Maples in the fall. Pages 20–21: The chapel in winter. Pages 22–23: Pyramid-shaped hornbeams along one of the garden allées. Pages 24–27: Overview of the Agnelli home at Villar Perosa and surrounding countryside. Pages 28–29: Snow covers the main house, including the lemon and magnolia terraces.*

Library of Congress Cataloging-in-Publication Data

Agnelli, Marella.
The Agnelli gardens at Villar Perosa : two centuries of a family retreat / by Marella Agnelli ;
essays by Marella Agnelli and Marella Caracciolo ; with commentaries by Paolo Pejrone.
p.   cm.
ISBN 0–8109–1979–6
1. Giardini Agnelli (Villar Perosa, Italy)—History.   2. Agnelli family—Homes and haunts—
Italy—Villar Perosa—History.   3. Giardini Agnelli (Villar Perosa, Italy)—Pictorial works.
4. Agnelli family—Homes and haunts—Italy—Villar Perosa—Pictorial works.   5. Agnelli family.
I. Caracciolo, Marella.   II. Pejrone, Paolo.   III. Title.
SB466.I83G4225   1998
712'.6'094512—DC21   98–7763

Printed and bound in Italy by Arti Grafiche Amilcare Pizzi S.p.A.

Harry N. Abrams, Inc.
100 Fifth Avenue
New York, N.Y. 10011
www.abramsbooks.com

Contents

Giacomo (James) Grosso (1860–1938). Villa Agnelli at Villar Perosa. *1921. Oil on cloth, 55⅞ x 72½ in.*

Introduction

Marella Agnelli

The desire to write the history of the Agnelli gardens at Villar Perosa, near Turin, originated in a conversation that took place several years ago in these same gardens with my niece, Marella Caracciolo, affectionately called Marellina. It was at sunset, on a particularly mild day in late September. We had just concluded our afternoon walk by going up to the balcony on the second floor of the villa and taking in the familiar shapes of the gardens before darkness fell. Everything was peaceful and still. The tidy, undulating lawn extended like a great green wave in front of us. From its center, a perfectly round fountain gave off the delicate sound of running water. Here and there gigantic shapes of ancient trees stood solemnly like statues: a small group of lindens, a sequoia, a large *Araucaria,* and a smaller one nearby. A massive *Olea fragrans* leaned its weight on one corner of the facade, its tiny white flowers releasing their sweetness into the air. Beyond the gardens, on the opposite side of the valley, the contours of the mountains were dissolving and becoming almost transparent, like a huge Japanese screen hanging in the evening light.

Urged on by Marellina's curiosity, I told her some stories about the villa and the gardens where we had just taken our walk. Although I was intimate with the trees, the paths—in fact, with nearly every flower—I was less familiar with the history of the place and the people who had lived here before me. So I started recounting what I could, beginning with my arrival at Villar Perosa in 1953.

I was newly married and, like Aniceta before me, I was enchanted by Villar. In those years it exuded a timeless aura, as if the entire villa was a sleeping beauty hidden in the woods. It exuded a refined tranquillity that went back to Clara's time. The villa's old servants, who were still a part of daily life, maintained the quiet customs and the slow rhythms of those days. Their easy manner and gentle presence had been instilled in them by the *senatore* in order to preserve his wife's serenity.

That evening on the balcony, I recalled the respectful kindness with which my husband and I had been welcomed more than thirty years earlier. I was the new Mrs. Agnelli. The servants showed us both such genuine kindness, complemented by the great dignity characteristic of the people who live in the mountains. Agostino Stella, the butler, was waiting for us at the entrance to the great stairway. Though gray haired, he stood erect with an impeccable style that was nearly military in its correctness. Once inside the hall, which was waxed to a perfect shine, Mina was introduced to me. She had been the personal maid of the "*senatrice,*" as they called Clara Boselli, wife of *senatore* Giovanni Agnelli. Standing next to Mina was Agnese, the maid in charge of the house linens. Agnese was the wife of the person who plays an important part in our story—the head gardener, Gaetano Aloisio.

Two elderly servants were wearing long, perfectly ironed aprons that came down to their ankles. Over these, they wore white, starched camisoles with finely embroidered bibs. Because of the warmth and courtesy shown us by the servants, I loved the house from that first moment. Together Gaetano and Agostino were the main custodians of a time gone by; they also proved to be patient and reliable narrators of our home.

All these things I enjoyed telling Marellina. By this time shadows had overtaken the garden. The formidable profiles of the trees stood out like shapes of cut velvet, reminding us of Aniceta.

The legendary Madame Aniceta Agnelli Lampugnani—mother of *senatore* Giovanni Agnelli, the founder of Fiat—was the true creator of the garden. After Aniceta there was the complex but influential figure of Clara Boselli Agnelli, wife of the *senatore*. Although Clara chose a rather solitary life at Villar, her vision of our home was handed down to her heirs. My mother-in-law, Virginia Bourbon del Monte, died young and did not have the time or the opportunity to leave a mark on Villar Perosa. And neither did Tina Agnelli Nasi.

Across the distance of time, portraits of other women, whose destinies were inextricably linked to Villar Perosa, came to life. There was, for example, the beautiful and sophisticated Marchioness Polissena Turinetti di Priero, who received the estate of Villar Perosa as a wedding gift from her father in 1781, and who probably designed the two eighteenth-century terraced gardens at the rear of the villa. An ardent patriot and fierce opponent of the French, Polissena was imprisoned in the fort of Fenestrelle by the emperor Napoleon himself before she was sent into exile. Then there was her daughter, Marchioness Clementina Incontri, painted by François-Xavier Fabre. Her premature death, in 1839, is remembered on the memorial stone at the entrance to a tiny red-brick chapel at the foot of the garden of Villa Agnelli.

As memories and anecdotes were revealed that late afternoon in September, the gardens of Villar Perosa gradually took on a new dimension. Along every path, behind every tree, we could feel the silent presence of these women whose minds and emotions had left a visible impression on the grounds. We became curious to find out more about them and in doing so to explore the origins of these gardens, in which, in succeeding periods, their individual destinies had met and communicated. Gardens, so receptive to influences, are a perfect metaphor for this communion between present and past.

From this point of view the Villar gardens are a particularly fascinating subject. They are a synthesis of many different minds and sensibilities, and their transformations, over the course of several generations, also mirror the evolution of the Agnelli family.

As it turned out, the research for this book proved more complicated than either of us had anticipated. First of all, there was the problem of the historical missing links regarding the origins of the villa itself. Although its design, or parts of it, has been attributed to the great architect Filippo Juvarra, there are no documents that can prove it conclusively. The villa's location is another mystery: why would anyone, in the second decade of the eighteenth century, have wanted to build such an extravagantly elegant summer home in a remote frontier territory burdened by a recent history of violent foreign invasions? Several elements suggest that the villa was originally intended to be a royal hunting lodge, a pleasurable alternative at the time to the harsh military life at the nearby forts. This too, however, has never been fully proved.

Another obstacle was the lack of Agnelli documents concerning Villar Perosa. Much energy was spent trying to locate at least some of the letters, personal diaries, and other private documents belonging to the women of the family. In them we hoped to find interesting references to the gardens. Unfortunately, we soon discovered that boxes and boxes of papers had been lost or destroyed in the course of several relocations. Other papers had been reduced to ashes during the air raids that, in January 1944, struck the two facing wings of Villa Agnelli where Aniceta, Clara, and Virginia had their bedrooms. In just seconds, what these women had accumulated in the course of their years at Villar Perosa—their books, diaries, letters, photographs, and personal objects—were all blown to pieces.

This void has been, paradoxically, a source of inspiration. It has led to a number of fascinating interviews with older members of the Agnelli family. Gianni Agnelli and his sisters, Clara, Susanna (known as Suni), and Maria Sole, have shared some of their childhood memories. Their cousins Clara Nasi and her younger sister Umberta have also been an invaluable source of information. Extensive research in public libraries and private archives has produced old documents, newspapers, magazines, biographies, and other written records that have proved essential to piecing together this remarkable story.

The greatest source of inspiration, however, the place one always returned to when there were too many missing pieces, has been the gardens themselves. Despite their many incarnations, the gardens of Villar Perosa remain faithful to their past. Polissena's terraced gardens and her rose red chapel are still there and so are traces of Aniceta's nineteenth-century taste, her passion for exotic trees and shady bowers. Clara's balcony, which her husband had built for her, and from which she would observe the world go by or enjoy the transparent mountain sunsets, is also part of the scene.

Russell Page's vision expanded the confines of the Agnelli gardens far beyond its ancient boundaries and into the surrounding landscape. He tried, not entirely successfully, to strip it of its old-fashioned, vaguely provincial quality. The result of these often conflicting visions is a vast park where an awe-inspiring setting, surrounded by dramatic views of the mountains, is balanced by a more intimate approach with many shady paths and ancient stone staircases leading to the discovery of well-loved and secret gardens.

The Story of the Garden

Marella Agnelli and Marella Caracciolo

The rugged and uneven landscape along the Chisone River is interrupted by cultivated fields, thick and shady woods, and embellished by charming houses situated on the hilltops that, to the east, border with the Waldensian valleys forming a magnificent amphitheatre along the edge of the torrent before receding into the Cottian Alps. . . .

On the top of a delightful hillock to the right of the road one can see a charming country house, the summer residence of a highly distinguished family. A beautiful dome, like that of a church, rises above the building, making it visible within the landscape from a distance.

The village of Perosa, with its church and its towers perched high on a sloping hill, overlooks the surrounding landscape as if it were a post of military observation.

—William Beattie, *The Waldenses or Protestant Valleys of Piedmont, Dauphiny and the Ban de la Roche,* 1836

The coachman cracked his whip and the horses cheerfully started off, stimulated by a delicate breeze in the dawn that was turning the Monviso silver. An excursion from Pinerolo to Fenestrelle, on such a beautiful, airy and clear day.

Above San Germano, we began to see a few Waldensian peasant women, with their clean little white bonnets, amid those charming hills, their slopes covered with grapevines, clothed in heather and beeches higher up, where the "little beards" climb at daybreak, books under their arms, to go to the itinerant master's school, amid the lonely hamlets of the peaks. And from that point on up we found the valley to be lively with those myriad scattered, slow sounds, of carts, herds, collar bells, and isolated smithies that caress the ear and calm the heart.

Here is Villar Perosa, host to kings, displaying amid the greenery its little bright white copy of the Basilica di Superga.

—Edmondo De Amicis, *Alle porte d'Italia,* 1884

Pinerolo is the regional capital. The torrential Chisone begins up in the Alpe Troncea, rushing down through the harsh, steep valley that bears its name. It arrives suddenly at a broad, vast tableland.

Here the stream, calmer now, begins to meander through fields of corn and rye, vineyards, and fruit trees. Here is Villar Perosa. High up on the left, the too large church overlooks the valley. Just below, Villa Agnelli can only be glimpsed, hidden by the greenery of its park.

Postcard of Villar Perosa around the turn of the century.

Leaving the tableland, the river resumes its precipitous course. The valley narrows again between leaden, shaded cliffs to Pinerolo. A former garrison, Pinerolo's fortified walls indicate a history of invasions from the north, especially France, which the people of this region have resisted, not always successfully. Pinerolo has, however, retained much of its graceful eighteenth-century architecture, some of it left by the French and some built during a period of prosperity resulting from expanded production of textiles and trade goods, chiefly silk.

Today Pinerolo, after its many past tribulations, is a peaceful little town. With the spacious fan of the Alps to the north, one can glimpse to the south, beyond the city, the broad and fertile expanses of the Pianura Padana (the Po Valley), which stretch for miles and miles, as far as the horizon.

Unlike the mountains framing it to the north, this endless stretch of flat, heavily industrialized and cultivated land appears monotonous. Poplar trees, planted in rows like sentries, mark the borders of fields and properties, occasionally interrupting the flatness of this valley that is fog drenched in winter and hot and humid in summer.

Turin, the city where the Agnellis have lived for at least six generations, was the heart and sum of Italy's unification. Beginning in 1889, and continuing today, it has also been the center of the nation's car industry. Office buildings, factories, and residential neighborhoods accommodate the population that, over the course of this century, has migrated to Turin to work. Though no longer *la plus jolie* of the cities of Europe, as French scholar Charles de Brosses described it in 1749, Turin is still a magnificent, mysterious city. The long straight streets, the tree-lined avenues, and the spacious squares surrounded by porticoes combine to endow the city with a sober, if somewhat predictable, elegance. The gray-blue waters of the Po River flow placidly through the center of the city, breaking the geometric regularity of the town plan.

Along a stretch of the river on the side opposite the city is what Torinesi commonly refer to as *la collina:*

View of the Villar Perosa villa with the church and the tower, early 1900s.

vast, thickly wooded hills, where in the course of the past two centuries many of the city's wealthier families have built their summer homes. Since the second half of the nineteen-sixties, Avvocato Gianni Agnelli and his wife, Donna Marella, have transformed one such villa, Frescot, into their town house.

At Villar Perosa, where for six generations the Agnelli family has come together for part of the summer, the air is clear and cool. The mountains enclosing the valley are dotted with stands of beeches, oaks, alders, hornbeams, and chestnut trees. A few terraced fields, carved laboriously from between the rocks of these mountains and planted with grapevines or fruit trees, especially apples and pears, testify to many centuries of a hard life.

Senatore Giovanni Agnelli, grandfather of Gianni and founder of Fiat (Fabbrica Italiana Automobili Torino), brought industrialization to the inhabitants of this valley during the first decade of this century. Since then, the population has increased significantly and become a middle-class community. Few of them, however, have lost the accent or direct manner that reveals their ancient Provençal roots. Industrialization and wealth have also been crucial to eradicating what remained of many centuries of religious prejudices between the local Catholic community and the Protestant one, the Waldensians. Indeed, for centuries Val Chisone was the setting for many battles and periods of religious persecution of the Waldensians.

The Waldensians are an ancient Protestant community that takes its name from Pierre Valdès, a late-twelfth-century merchant from Lyons who preached poverty and a life based upon a strict reading of the Gospels as the only means to spiritual salvation. Escaping violent persecution in Provence, the Waldensians originally found refuge among these mountains during the thirteenth century. After an initial period of relative peace, they were subsequently persecuted by the local Catholics as well and forced to retreat to the remotest areas of the mountains. As the centuries passed, the battles became so fierce and persistent that at one point in the 1680s the Waldensians had no choice but to seek refuge across the border in Switzerland. From there they returned, about three years later, to their beloved mountains of Piedmont, in a heroic journey that entered history as *la glorieuse rentrée,* the glorious return home.

The Waldensians were finally granted political and civil rights by King Carlo Alberto of Sardinia in 1848. But as early as the late eighteenth century, the many tales of their misfortunes and stoic opposition to the Catholic persecution had already attracted the notice of northern European travelers and writers.

Today Val Chisone is defined as much by its industry as by its picturesque mountains. Its heart is a complex of industrial buildings, some of which date back to the first years of this century. In one of these, *senatore* Agnelli in 1906 headquartered R.I.V., the first Italian ball bearings factory. The many little white two-story houses, each surrounded by its walled garden, edging the straight streets of the little town of Villar Perosa bear testimony to Agnelli's grand vision. With its factories, schools, hospitals, library, and churches, Villar Perosa became, by the late twenties, the model in Italy of a small industrial community.

From the state highway that goes from Turin to the mountains, there is a small road on the right that edges the village of Villar Perosa, and which, after passing some houses and a children's playground, leads to the main square, Piazza Giovanni Agnelli, where the town hall is situated. A few elderly people are sitting, as always, in the shade of a small portico on one side of the square. A large bronze statue of Giovanni Agnelli, a tribute on the part of Agnelli's townspeople, was erected in 1970 directly in front of the town hall, and it symbolically marks the entrance to the site of the Agnelli family origins.

The road continues uphill past another small cluster of houses. A large iron-and-stone enclosure, bordering the right side of the road, marks the boundary of the Agnelli property. A long straight avenue flanked by huge ancient horse chestnut trees stretches beyond an iron gate. This is the main entrance, quite formal, which nonetheless is almost always closed, unlike a more discreet entrance a little farther along. The road con-

The facade of the villa at the beginning of the century.

39

tinues in a wide curve until there appear orchards, vineyards, and other crops punctuated by a series of large hornbeams on both sides of the road.

This avenue, narrower than the first, was conceived, around the mid-fifties, by the British landscape designer Russell Page as the secondary entrance to a garden in which a sense of tended beauty and a wild, dramatic landscape have been successfully combined into a unique visual experience. No detail within the boundaries of the Agnelli property has seemingly been left to chance or to nature alone.

Higher up the hill that overlooks the park is the Church of San Pietro in Vincoli. An example of Piedmontese Baroque architecture, it was built between 1711 and 1718 and, like the villa, has often been attributed to Juvarra. With its dominant situation, the church's two bell towers, great copper dome, and the light ocher tones of its plaster walls all make it look as if it was intended to unequivocally mark the Catholic presence on this tableland and on this sunny side of the valley and to be seen by the Waldensian communities holed up in the tiny Alpine villages on the opposite side of the freezing northern slopes.

The Gardens

At the end of the avenue of the large hornbeams, instead of continuing left toward the Church of San Pietro in Vincoli, go straight and enter through a simple gate into the gardens.

The immediate impression is one of solemnity. A gigantic *Araucaria*, a few sequoias, a cluster of old lindens, and other huge trees are, with the villa, the absolute stars of the estate. Their contrasting natures—separate, massive, and ancient—impart to this area of the gardens a special atmosphere. This is a part of the natural, or English-style, garden that Aniceta brought into being.

In the shade of these trees, a great lawn stretches from the villa's facade as far as the avenues leading into the estate. Its undulating surface, patchy with the shade of the various trees, gives a sense of irregular movement that complements and contrasts with the formality of the villa. This feeling of surprise and contrast is emphasized by the presence of a Neo-Gothic tower. And next to it, half hidden by a tall and overgrown hedge of boxwood and yew, is the facade of a tiny red stucco chapel that stands out like a jewel among the surrounding green.

In the middle of the great lawn is a vast mirror of round water. It is bordered not by stones but by the neatly clipped grass. Nor are there any decorative elements except for a single jet rising in the center. Like many areas of the gardens, the fountain was redesigned and simplified by Page and Marella Agnelli to replace an earlier and much more elaborate version.

An ample and free sense of space is what best defines this part of the gardens. Although once inside the estate one feels light-years away from the surrounding world—the village, the factories, the busy road carrying vacationers up to the hills of Sestriere—there is a sense of great openness, provided especially by the views of the surrounding mountains. This feeling of space and mystery is also hinted at through occasional glimpses of shady avenues and paths leading to other areas of this vast park.

The Villa

Villa Agnelli—called "il castello" (the castle) by the locals, perhaps in memory of a fortress or outpost—is a particularly successful example of Piedmontese Baroque architecture. This style, characterized by light and graceful contours, resurfaced in the second decade of the eighteenth century as a reaction to the devastating invasion of 1706, when the French set fire to and destroyed some of the region's most beautiful villas. The constant fear in this border area of foreign invasions has infused the history of this country house with a mystery unique to its location. Though there are no documents to prove it, many historians believe the villa was originally intended as a hunting lodge for Vittorio Amedeo II, duke of Savoy and king of Sardinia. The fact that he was obliged to spend much of his time in Val Chisone, at the military outposts of the nearby fort of Fenestrelle, seems to support this theory.

The property of Villar Perosa, together with other estates, was granted in the early years of the eighteenth century by Vittorio Amedeo II, then its owner, to the three Piccon brothers, in exchange for other properties that they were forced to give back to the Waldensian community. This was during a truce and perhaps also meant to pay back some of the royal debts, a constant for the house of Savoy, and especially for Vittorio Amedeo II. One of the three brothers, Count Luigi Piccon, personally oversaw the construction of the Church of San Pietro in Vincoli and the villa at the same time. After their completion, Count Piccon embarked on a long and exhausting lawsuit against the local population in order to try to set exclusive hunting rights on the property. We suspect that in this instance too, Piccon may have been acting on behalf of his king, whose passion for hunting was legendary.

What historians do know is that King Carlo Emanuele III, who dethroned and imprisoned his father, Vittorio Amedeo II, in 1730 (ironically, he arrested his father with the help of Luigi Piccon), would often stop at Villar Perosa during his frequent hunting expeditions on the mountains or en route to inspect the nearby fort of Fenestrelle.

Attached to the left corner of the original main building is a more recent structure called the *palazzina dei bambini*—the children's cottage. From the outside, the square, entirely ivy-covered structure conveys a sober demeanor that in no way lessens the villa's beauty. Built in the 1920s by *senatore* Agnelli to create more space and accommodate a continually growing family, the interiors of this cottage have retained a charming feeling of childhood. From the entrance hall, a wooden staircase leads to the second floor and the children's playrooms and bedrooms. Everything in these rooms—from the large stuffed tiger in the main room to the brick red

The "Chinese" gallery on the first floor of the villa.

linoleum floors, from the rooms with flowered wallpaper to the family portraits, and even the spacious bathrooms with the original porcelain tubs—takes us back to the period between the world wars.

The villa itself is rather different in its structure, decoration, and, of course, its atmosphere. The gallery on the ground floor probably goes back to a previous building. Its proportions are quite different from those of the gallery on the first floor, which is open and spacious with stucco decorations everywhere. The two galleries are linked by a grand stairway, which seems a smaller but more graceful version of the one in Palazzo Madama in Turin.

> *This stairway and the gallery that leads to it take up the entire central part of the house, on the side where the entrance is. With their simple magnificence, they reinforce the building's claim to royal origins and prepare the visitor for the surprises of the interior.*
>
> *The French architectural phrase* maison de lanterne *defines the character of the villa very well. It does not resemble a lantern in the sense that it is open on all sides; in fact, many rooms are quite intimate and some are not well lit. But it is rather a house that opens up in many places. As one walks through it, one almost seems to be out in the open in the verandas or between the spacious windows. For example, those of the main stairway convey a sensation of being suspended in the air as if in a bird cage.*
>
> —Nigel Nicholson, *Great Houses*

Thanks to the nearby location of the port of Genoa, which traded with the Far East, chinoiseries had become extremely fashionable in Piedmont as well, and Chinese wallpaper in particular. Since it was too expensive to paper the entire gallery, the owners of Villa Agnelli made do with craftsmen from the local area and the nearby mountains—as was done also in the hunting lodge of Stupinigi designed by Juvarra.

The interiors of the main villa have an altogether more sophisticated allure. On the ground floor a succession of spacious rooms opens onto stunning views of the front and back gardens. The main hallway, which was probably an old stable once, has beautiful vaulted ceilings suggestive of late-seventeenth-century architecture. Exquisite stucco decorations trace the contours of walls and ceilings with patterns that suggest the delicacy of ancient lace. The names of some of the rooms, Sala Giardino, Sala Vescovo, Sala Vescovessa, add to the overall feeling of order.

From the elongated central hallway one gains access to the Juvarresque staircase. This leads to the loggia above, originally designed to remain open throughout the year, but enclosed by glass windows in the late nineteenth century. A large opening leads to the so-called Chinese gallery. This long, narrow room is decorated with painted scenes in the Chinese style that became increasingly fashionable in Piedmont after the 1730s.

In one of the rooms opening onto the gallery is a charming portrait of a young woman, Clementina Turinetti (later, Marchioness Incontri), seated in a mysterious, timeless wooded landscape. At her feet a dog wears a collar on which is engraved the family name Prié. In the background of the painting, beyond a dense cover of dark leaves, mountains can be glimpsed in the distance. An indirect gesture, perhaps, to the family's Piedmontese and mountain origins.

This portrait was commissioned by Marchioness Polissena Turinetti del Prié (di Priero) from the French painter François-Xavier Fabre, who finished it in 1803. The name of Polissena Turinetti, so prominent in the history of Villar Perosa, conjures up the image of a beautiful and fascinating woman of character. Polissena was the only child of Count Gamba della Perosa e del Villar, a wealthy banker from Moncalieri, near Turin. He bought the Villar estate between 1758 and 1760, and this is where Polissena spent many summers. In 1781, when she married Marquess Giovanni Antonio Turinetti, who belonged to one of the most prominent families of Piedmont, she was given Villar Perosa as part of her dowry.

After her wedding, Polissena continued to spend a part of every summer at Villar Perosa, and despite the many other properties belonging to Turinetti di Priero, she considered this to be her true home.

Polissena must have enjoyed gardening. It was probably she who commissioned the two terraced gardens behind the house. Although these terraces were redesigned in the second half of the nineteenth century, the architectural structure has retained faint traces of its original eighteenth-century formality. A stone staircase unites the closer terrace to the one a little farther up, where, somewhat more recently, magnolia trees have been planted.

A guide to Pinerolo and the surrounding region, published in 1800, describes the villa as a "magnificent building" located in "a delightful district and the largest and most enchanting part" of Val Chisone. The guide also mentions the presence of a garden composed according to the "modern taste of the period." This

François-Xavier Fabre (1766–1837). Clementina Incontri,
Marquise of Prié (1786–1839). *Oil on cloth, 26 x 19⅝ in.*

reference to the garden suggests that Polissena Turinetti had made several changes and that she therefore planned to dedicate some of her time to the Villar Perosa property.

These projects were cut short in 1792–93 by the war with France. At that time Marquess Giovanni Turinetti, Polissena's husband and, like her, an impassioned patriot, sided with the king of Sardinia. Following the French invasion, Polissena decided to leave Turin with her children. Her husband, who stayed behind, was later accused of having plotted against the invading government and arrested by the French police in 1794. After a period of imprisonment, Marquess Turinetti was forced to leave Piedmont and live some years in exile, first in Grenoble and subsequently in Dijon and Autun. Polissena pleaded incessantly with the French authorities for the return of her husband and finally, in 1801, Napoleon granted clemency to Giovanni, who was free to return to his family. This turned out to be a short-lived happiness: Giovanni Turinetti died, in Turin, just a few months after his return.

After the death of her husband, Polissena decided to leave both Turin and Villar Perosa once again and repair to Florence for a few months before settling in Rome. Her sojourn in Tuscany was recorded by her friend the duchess of Albany in her diary: "The Marchioness of Prié has put her children in a boarding school in Siena and has gone on to Rome where she will reside for a time."

Polissena spent almost five years in exile, mostly in Rome, where, according to the distinguished historian of the subalpine aristocracy, Antonio Manno, this "beautiful and magnificent woman" continued to plot against the French. It was during this period in exile that she met the painter Fabre, who was also an ardent opponent of the new French regime, and who lived in exile in Italy.

It is uncertain what happened to Villar during all those years. Most likely the villa was closed, as was common in those troubled times, and the fields rented out. Perhaps, like other properties in Piedmont, the villa of Villar Perosa was temporarily occupied by French authorities. What is known is that in 1806, following certain financial difficulties and increasingly anxious to regain possession of her properties, Polissena Turinetti decided to return to Turin with her daughter Clementina. The presence of Marchioness Turinetti, however, did not go unnoticed by the Napoleonic authorities, who placed her and those who met in her salon under close surveillance. Within a year the French had found enough grounds to justify her arrest. Many years later Polissena's nephew Massimo d'Azeglio would write that "The Marchioness of Prié, my aunt, an agreeable, spirited and energetic woman, who knew her way in political and social affairs, so fervently hated the French changes that Napoleon himself considered her presence a threat and had her sent to Fenestrelle."

After a brief period spent in the dark dungeons of this mountain fort, not far away from Villar Perosa, Polissena and her daughter were obliged to resume their life as political exiles. This time they headed north, to Paris, where Clementina married Marquess Lodovico Incontri, Bali of the Order of Malta, in 1809.

A few years later Polissena's forced exile was revoked. The Turinetti family palace in Turin, however, remained forfeit to the French authorities. Other estates were sold or rented in an attempt to relieve the family's increasingly precarious financial situation. It was at this point, it seems, that the destinies of the Turinetti di Priero and of the Agnelli family came together in Villar Perosa. Beginning in the second decade of the nineteenth century, Giuseppe Francesco Agnelli, a young cavalry officer with entrepreneurial ambitions in agriculture and the raising of silkworms, rented some of the Villar field and, at a later date, bought the villa.

Beginnings

What I have always heard in the family is that my grandfather's grandfather, like many Piedmontese officers of his generation, returned a richer man after having fought the Russian campaigns with Napoleon. Tired of the military life, he decided to embark on a new adventure, at Villar.

—Gianni Agnelli, Villa Frescot, Turin

Villa Frescot, Turin. It is a damp, gray afternoon in late April 1997. Although spring is near, a wintry grayness still hangs over the surrounding landscape and the city at the foot of the hill. A soft rain has been drizzling down continuously for the past two or three days from the dark sky and gives the vegetation a well-nourished luster.

From the tall windows of the living room in this lovely mid-eighteenth-century mansion, one can catch a few glimpses of the new, round leaves of the persimmon trees that grow amid flower beds filled with red cin-cin roses in one of the terraced gardens surrounding the villa. Like Villar Perosa, the garden of Villa Frescot is the result of a collaborative effort between Marella Agnelli and Russell Page.

On this particular afternoon a small group of people has gathered together for a cup of tea and a friendly chat in the main living room of the villa. Marchesa Clara Nasi Ferrero, of Ventimiglia, a sharp-witted woman around eighty years old, and her younger sister, Signora Umberta Nasi Ajmone Marsan, have come to Villa Frescot to share some of their childhood recollections of Villar Perosa. Their mother, Tina Agnelli Nasi, who died at a young age a few days after giving birth to her fifth child, was the only daughter of *senatore* Agnelli and his wife, Clara.

Like their Agnelli cousins, the Nasi children spent many summers with their grandparents at Villar Perosa during the twenties and thirties. Their recollections have been very helpful in re-creating the atmosphere in the house during those years. Just as the two sisters are preparing to leave after an afternoon spent among old photographs and fascinating stories, the door to the living room opens and their cousin Gianni Agnelli, l'avvocato, walks in.

Despite his seventy-six years of age, Gianni Agnelli has managed to retain his vitality and his well-known and much extolled charisma. In the living room, he greets Clara and Umberta affectionately and then studies some old photographs that show him as a child at Villar, along with his many brothers and cousins. A few minutes later, his cousins having taken their leave, *l'avvocato* adds some details about his family history and Villar Perosa.

"I have always heard," he says, "that Villar Perosa was acquired by my grandfather's grandfather, Giuseppe Francesco Agnelli, on his return from the Russian campaigns." He goes on to explain that like many Piedmontese cavalry officers, Giuseppe Francesco had followed Napoleon and the French army to Russia and had returned richer than he had left. "After these harsh wars, however," *l'avvocato* Agnelli continues, "though still a young man, he decided to retire from a military career and invest the capital he had earned in a new adventure: land." That is how the Agnelli forebear became interested in land and farming and started renting large plots in the Val Chisone area as well. "I don't think Giuseppe Francesco was particularly interested in agriculture as such," Gianni Agnelli explains. "What interested him were the mulberry trees for raising silkworms. The production of silk was still, at that time, one of the major industries of this region. That, I think, is how he started his fortune. At Villar Perosa, however, Giuseppe Francesco also cultivated apple trees to make cider."

Exactly when Giuseppe Francesco arrived at Villar Perosa remains, to this day, an open question. Gianni

Agnelli maintains that his ancestor bought Villar in 1811, a version endorsed by other family members. The public documents, however, indicate that the actual date of acquisition took place quite a few years later, in 1853—a gap of more than forty years to be accounted for.

One possible interpretation is that although Giuseppe Francesco Agnelli did indeed arrive at Villar Perosa soon after the Napoleonic wars, at the beginning he only rented lands to farm the crops that interested him. This would help explain several questions, including why Marchioness Polissena Turinetti and her children hardly ever went to Villar after their return to Piedmont in 1811. Their prolonged absence was noted by the local parish priest, who, in a number of letters replying to Polissena's numerous requests to build a chapel on the grounds of Villar Perosa, answered in offended tones that the "Marchesi di Priero" were never there, and so, in his opinion, the construction of a private chapel ought not to be approved.

Polissena Turinetti herself, in a letter dated April 27, 1844, expressed her desire to be buried in what she called her "former estate"—Villar Perosa. The phrase "former estate" reveals that at least nine years before the official sale, Polissena no longer considered the land and the villa her personal property. This inconsistency can be explained only by the fact that the Turinettis had already been leasing the property for some time to permanent tenants: the Agnellis.

Who was this enterprising cavalry veteran, barely twenty-one years old? In a well-researched dissertation on the genealogy of the Agnelli family, written by Gustavo Mola di Nomaglio, Giuseppe Francesco Agnelli is described as a "banker entrepreneur of proto-industrial Piedmont," who, while remaining somewhat involved with trade and agriculture, at the same time energetically promoted the industrial innovations of his times.

Let us back up a step. Giuseppe Francesco Agnelli was born in the town of Racconigi, in Piedmont, on June 25, 1789. He was the youngest of twelve children of a middle-class family and as such would have had little, if any, help or hereditary rights.

At an early age, at least by modern standards, Giuseppe Francesco left his family and went his own way. Following a brief period in battle, he became involved in silk production, which may have subsequently led him to expand his investments into the spice trade. Documents published in the 1820s describe him as a wealthy merchant, and from 1830 his name would be published alongside those of the most important "Turinese bankers and silk traders."

In 1821 Giuseppe Francesco married a young widow, Anna Maria Maggia. The couple settled in Turin. Though they had two children, Edoardo and Carola, theirs was not a happy marriage, and in 1838 they filed for separation.

By the time Giuseppe Francesco bought Villar Perosa in 1853, he had been separated from his wife for more than fifteen years; after her death, Agnelli married Irene Benevelli, about whom little is known. The acquisition of Villar took place shortly after Giuseppe Francesco sold another of his large properties, in the village of

Candiolo. There were two main reasons that had induced him to buy Villar Perosa from the Turinetti family. First, he saw it as a good business opportunity. Second, he was undoubtedly attracted by the idea of owning this estate because of its association with important royal figures in Piedmontese history. He certainly understood that by possessing Villar Perosa he would inevitably elevate the social status of his family.

In those years the Agnelli family used the villa only in the summer months. Photographs taken in the late nineteenth century show that the stairway from the ground floor to the second floor in front was completely open, which would certainly have made it difficult to live in the villa during the cold months. Other than that, judging from the photos, the main villa looked very much as it does today. In a geographic dictionary of Piedmont published in 1854, less than a year after Agnelli acquired Villar, one reads: "Here is a superb summer residence with a magnificent mansion and a garden in the modern fashion. It is located in a very pleasant area, in the most spacious and delightful area of the Perosa valley. The facade of the mansion is modeled on that of Palazzo Madama in Turin."

The garden of Villar in the days of Giuseppe Francesco Agnelli was much smaller than it is now, comprising a couple of acres in total, given the lawns, flower beds, and various terraced gardens. The long and narrow south-facing terraces were used for kitchen gardens, vineyards, and fruit trees.

A drawing of Villar Perosa by Clemente Rovere is interesting because it shows a portion of the front garden as it was around 1847, before the Agnelli family officially owned the property. In the drawing we see a view of the tower from the house. Surrounded by a thick growth of trees, mostly beech and fir trees, the tower suggests a folly in the English taste. Informal plantings add a romantic touch. A winding path marks the way from the front of the villa to the garden entrance, a gate very much like the present one and, to judge from the drawing, situated a little beyond the tower.

After the acquisition of Villar Perosa, the Agnellis became the most influential family in the Val Chisone and one of the first families in the Pinerolo region. In many ways they replaced the ancient landowners in the eyes of the locals. Not only did the Agnellis live in *il castello,* but, beginning with Giuseppe Francesco, the head of the Agnelli family in every generation to come took on important roles in the community.

Aniceta's Garden

Aniceta Frisetti, my grandfather's mother, was an intelligent, energetic, and witty woman. It was she who guided my grandfather in his youth, and rather strictly. She was unsentimental but had a great passion for gardening. In Villar Perosa she slept in a room on the second floor that looked onto the terraces at the rear of the house and from these directly over the garden.

—Clara Nasi, Villa Frescot, Turin

Portrait of Aniceta Agnelli made during the time of her second marriage to Luigi (Louis) Lampugnani (1882).

On the top floor of Villa Agnelli at Villar Perosa is a guest room that opens onto a long balcony overlooking the Church of San Pietro in Vincoli and the garden at the back of the house. Called the "blue hydrangeas" room, it is named after the floral patterns on the walls. Unlike many other rooms in Villar, which have retained a more late-eighteenth- or early-nineteenth-century atmosphere, this room is characterized by the ample proportions of its late-nineteenth-century furniture. Each piece, from the large double bed to the slightly convex armoire and the chest of drawers by the door, was embellished and personalized with a curly capital "A" carved into the wood. As it turns, out the "A" stands not only for Agnelli but also for Aniceta, the first name of one of the most influential women in this story.

When Aniceta Frisetti entered the Agnelli family as a young bride in 1865, she was a cheerful nineteen-year-old who took pleasure in socializing. The dowry she brought to the marriage further allowed her this kind of freedom. Her marriage to Edoardo Agnelli, Giuseppe Francesco's only son, marked the beginning of a new era not only for the Agnelli family but especially for the development of the garden at Villar Perosa.

Aniceta came from a family background very similar to that of her husband. Like the Agnellis, the Frisetti family belonged to the emerging educated and wealthy upper middle class, which, with the advent of the industrial age, was becoming increasingly powerful both politically and socially. Aniceta's father, Giovanni Frisetti, was a successful financier who owned a large construction firm. He was also a friend and business partner of Giuseppe Francesco Agnelli. From many points of view, therefore, the Agnelli–Frisetti marriage was a desirable match.

The young couple settled in a large and comfortable house, built by the Ingeniere Frisetti, in a residential street in the center of Turin. In the years following the unification of Italy, Turin was experiencing many

A partial view of Villar Perosa when it was largely still an agricultural property.

exciting changes. As the capital of the new kingdom, it had become a thriving cultural and political center and industrial stronghold, thus attracting a great number of immigrants from many other regions of Italy.

In this atmosphere of euphoria and new social responsibilities, Edoardo and Aniceta soon made a name for themselves as some of the most active participants in the city's cultural and social life, despite their youth. They gave dinners and parties, participated enthusiastically in various charity events, and often went to the opera and the theater. Their names appear constantly in the gossip columns of the time. After his father's death in 1866, Edoardo, a sensitive and cultivated man, assumed more responsibility for the family business. At the same time, however, he managed to devote time and money to one of his passions: promoting and sponsoring the Society of Fine Arts.

Despite the enthusiasm with which they participated in their social activities in Turin, Edoardo and Aniceta managed to spend a few months each year in Villar Perosa. It was at Villar that their son, Giovanni, the future founder of Fiat, was born, in one of the second-floor rooms with high stuccoed ceilings and "Chinese" decorations overlooking the open loggias at the back of the villa. The date was August 13, 1866. His godparents, as we read in the baptismal documents kept in the archives of the local parish, were his maternal grandparents. A little sister, Felicita Carola, was born in Villar Perosa on November 3, 1869, a date indicating that the Agnellis, unlike others in the past who had used the villa only as a summer residence, liked to spend time there even during the cooler seasons.

The reason they stayed at the country house more was simple: Aniceta had fallen in love with Villar Perosa. She loved its magnificence, steeped in exquisitely aristocratic history, and, as the intelligent woman she was, she appreciated its symbolic value, which added to the family's prestige. By this time, the local people had come to regard the role of the Agnellis with respect and as the natural evolution of a long line of landowners.

Edoardo was elected mayor in 1865. Indeed, soon the Agnelli lifestyle had become so grand that whenever Edoardo and Aniceta went to Villar Perosa from Turin they would find a small group of servants ready to wait on them: a manservant, a linen maid, a nursemaid to assist the children's nanny, a cleaning woman, and, of course, a gardener.

It was the garden, more than the house, that preoccupied Aniceta, an interest that over time became a passion and, later still, a source of much pride. She saw that the garden required care, and also saw in it a potential for change and an opportunity to leave her mark. The garden at Villar had in fact remained virtually untouched since the time of Polissena Turinetti. Although there had been a gardener to take care of it during the era of Giuseppe Francesco, for many years no one had tried to restore the original design or give it a creative direction. Many areas, such as the one surrounding the tower at the end of the garden, were overgrown while others, like the terraces in the rear of the house, were in desperate need of attention and care.

With no fully formed plan, Aniceta began by planting a number of trees on the front lawn. Unfortunately, these first garden projects were cut short by two tragedies that struck the young Agnelli family in 1871. In February her one-year-old daughter, Felicita Carola, died of an illness. Some months later, in November, Edoardo, Aniceta's husband and little Giovanni's father, also died. He was just forty years old.

At the age of five, Giovanni Agnelli was sole heir to his father's fortune. Aniceta suddenly found herself, at the age of twenty-five, the single mother of a small child. She also became responsible for the administration of what remained of the Agnelli fortune, including the part that was her dowry.

Clara Nasi Ferrero, Aniceta's eldest great-granddaughter, was born in 1913 and was seven years old when her great-grandmother died, but she still has vivid memories of the time she spent at Aniceta's house during an epidemic of scarlet fever in 1919, which had infected some of her younger brothers and sisters. "She was a very likable and intelligent woman," Marchioness Ferrero explains, "but she was not given to displays of emotion. When we children went to visit her, she never put up with fusses or whining. She was our great-grandmother, but she never let herself go with cuddles or effusive affection with us grandchildren. I think she considered them ill-bred displays."

In the decades following the death of her husband, Aniceta never resumed the fashionable city social life that she had been used to, even when her years of formal mourning were over. Little Carola's sudden death, followed by the no less unexpected death of her husband, to whom she was deeply attached and who she felt had been her support and her companion, had shaken her profoundly. Her home was shattered.

In her despair she sought comfort in religion, a faith that was to shape her future life as well. Because she was a practical, active woman, Aniceta turned her energy to charitable works. Thus, she returned to her commitments as a public benefactor, at Villar Perosa as well as in Turin.

In the 1870s, after having been stripped of its role as the capital of Italy, Turin experienced a profound economic and cultural crisis. Despite the economic expansion of the 1860s, there were increasing numbers of unemployed, poor, and demoralized people. In a popular bimonthly magazine of the period called *La Donna* and published in Turin, Aniceta Agnelli's name appears many times at the head of lists of benefactresses to numerous charitable organizations. Over the course of her long life, in fact, Aniceta gave money and time to different organizations. She was one of the patronesses of the Ospedale Infantile Regina Margherita (Queen Margherita Children's Hospital) and patroness of the Cucina Malati Poveri (Soup Kitchen of the Sick and Poor), with the "goal of providing at no cost broth, bread, meat, wine, milk, eggs, and marsala to the poor and sick or convalescent." Aniceta's name was listed immediately below that of the honorary president, the duchess of Aosta, Princess Laetitia di Savoia Napoleone. Aniceta was on the board of the Scuola della Buona Massaia (the School of the Good Housewife), whose aim was to "teach working-class women at no cost all that they need to know in order to become good housewives." Then there were the Alpine summer camps, providing the children of needy families with vacations in the mountains. The charitable organizations in which Aniceta appears to have been most active, however, had to do with the education of women and their consequent economic independence. For example, she chaired an annual exhibition of women's arts and crafts, which she also promoted. (Aniceta herself excelled at embroidery and knitting.)

With the Opera Pia Lotteri, she contributed financially and personally in order to "provide for the convalescence of poor women and especially for girls with neither homes nor families, coming out of hospitals for acute and common illnesses that are neither contagious nor chronic, so that they might within a month finish their course of treatment and be restored to health, at no cost."

In the meantime, Giovanni had grown to school age. In 1873, about two years after his father's death, when Giovanni was little more than six years old, Aniceta enrolled him in the strict and well-regarded Collegio di San Giuseppe, run by the Fratelli delle Scuole Christiane (Brothers of the Christian Schools). For several generations, this very traditional school had been providing an elitist and strict education to the sons of the families of the aristocracy and the emerging upper middle class. Aniceta meant for her little son to follow a course of classical studies. Giovanni went as a day student to the *scuole,* where he was assigned the number 153, a distinctive number that he would have all of his student days there.

When he finished high school, in 1883, he left the *Collegio* for the military academy in Modena. It seems to have been Aniceta who wanted her son to follow a military career in the cavalry, considered to be extremely prestigious in the Piedmont of those days. She had always been proud of her only son. They loved and understood each other. Despite their deep understanding of each other, however, Aniceta does not appear to have been a particularly permissive or indulgent mother.

At the beginning of every summer, when the San Giuseppe school term was over, Aniceta and the then small Giovanni had traveled from Turin up the already hot plain to Pinerolo. A cart carried everything they needed for their stay until harvest time. The horse-drawn carriage went ahead. From Pinerolo they took the "Fort Road" up to the Villar tableland. The cool of the woods and the high mountains all around soon caused them to forget the sultry city air. In addition, the villa's thick walls and open loggias would complete the sense of well-being.

As time passed, Aniceta wholeheartedly took on the responsibility as head of the family and administrator of its holdings. Practical woman that she was, however, Aniceta never confused her pleasure in the place with idleness and vacation. On the contrary—her stays at Villar were practical, justified by supervising with increasing confidence the farms and agricultural plants. Her aim was to ensure that Villar would be self-supporting and produce a significant annual income. Also at that time there were grapevines that produced what the locals called "black wine," which was—according to Gianni Agnelli, who tried it—a particularly crude wine. There were also mulberry groves for the silkworms and apple orchards for making cider.

Naturally enough, this attention to agriculture carried over into the garden. According to the stories of an elderly gardener whose grandfather, also a gardener, worked for Aniceta for many years, hay was grown on the eighteenth-century terraces, which Aniceta remodeled in the late nineteenth century, at the back of the house; today these terraces have beds of roses and other cutting flowers. Then there were the many fruit orchards near the garden, like the pear and apple trees planted in rows along the two long, narrow terraces below the east wing of the villa, where Italian-style gardens were later planted. There was also a splendid vegetable garden, near the lower courtyard, which was one of Aniceta's great passions. Rows and rows of vegetables, various herbs, and salad greens grew in abundance for years. Gianni Agnelli's sister Suni Agnelli still remembers with pleasure how she and her siblings and cousins loved to spend time in that garden in the early thirties, reading or simply sitting together in the shade of a huge plum tree eating its small, sweet, just-picked fruit.

Spending the long summer months on the property, Aniceta little by little became skilled at administering the fields and farms. She also began giving much more time and attention to the garden, which soon blossomed into a passion. Her affection for Villar—and especially the grounds—began in the early days of her marriage and lasted all her long life.

Aniceta's adventurous spirit and enthusiasm inspired the transformation she was undertaking. The intrepid Aniceta had no counsel save her own taste and imagination. There was no landscape architect, as in our time, and no "garden designer," as Russell Page liked to style himself. There was not even a real gardener at the Villar of that time, only laborers skilled in looking after the fields, whom Aniceta recruited from the farms to help her in her new projects. She turned herself into a gardener. Aniceta was the one who organized, created, and experienced everything, and it was she who dreamed, placed, planted, joined, and divided.

As she became familiar with plants, Aniceta learned a few things that were essential to a good harvest. She was shrewd and careful in these matters too. She learned why some plants prospered while others did not, and the reasons for certain diseases and incidences of mortality. She became an expert on pruning and on how to have the soil prepared and fertilized. Mainly, however, she learned how important the ingredients of water, sun, and God were to healthy plants.

Her gardening fervor and constant attention led her to undertake a whole series of transformations of the site, which she pursued more by instinct than by planning. The villa, unlike other hunting lodges of the period, did not have the usual flat, formal facade. This served Aniceta in her first efforts.

The natural, or English-style, garden, as it was called, had by then taken over all of Europe, often replacing earlier, older designs based on classical geometric plans, box parterres, and other formal spaces. At Villar, there were no formal gardens for Aniceta to change or uproot. The space in which she practiced, and that became her own garden, began up high, where the great church rose, including grapevines, shady slopes, and a few terraces, which probably had been under cultivation. The lawn naturally made its way up to the loggias.

One day, Aniceta had the courage to plant a cedar of Lebanon in front of the house next to some beeches that were already there; it was followed the next year by a second one. Today, both trees occupy the south side of the main villa, their immense, shady, and dark masses towering. This is how Aniceta's English garden began.

No sooner had she tamed the house's immediate surroundings in this fashion than she turned her fancy toward an exotic dream. Typical at this time were great natural-science expeditions that returned with thousands of plants from afar. These new and exotic plants were soon used both in the name of science and for pleasure. Aniceta's dream was to use these new plants at Villar—it was a decision that involved risk and stubbornness (something she would pass on to little Giovanni), but she held fast. Hers was an adventurous spirit—a necessary ingredient for establishing an exotic arboretum in the Alps, with the help of a small group of peasants. Naturally, Aniceta had some failures, but given her indomitable character, these only caused her to try again, rather than to give up. Besides huge beeches and lindens, today we find in front of the house *Araucarias,* sequoias, catalpas, and certain species of Japanese maples.

What we do not find now, however, are various species of palm trees, in particular the *Cameron Cocus Phoenix* that Aniceta loved passionately and that were planted variously around the house. In the area where the children's cottage was later built, next to a former, very old washhouse, Aniceta also planted a small bamboo forest.

A specially elaborate treatment, repeated every year in early spring, was reserved for the borders that ran along the villa's facade. This consisted of filling two large earthenware pots with short palm trees with rather broad, soft leaves and placing them at the two corners of the main entrance of the villa. In front of these vases, borders of bright flowers, including ordinary scarlet sage and what is commonly known as erba luisa, or *Lippia citriodora,* were planted. The pots were then painted white so that they would blend in with the exterior wall of the building. Every year in early spring, after the last winter snows had melted and the first buds were about to show, Aniceta would tell the gardeners to get large pieces of coal and dip them into some fresh whitewash; when they were dry, these were elaborately arranged around the pots and borders as if part of a "natural" low wall of bright white stones. The gardener continued this decorative quirk, perhaps in dubious taste, even after

View to the east; the palm trees ordered by Aniceta can be seen here.

Aniceta died; it was discontinued only when the coal-fired heating system and coal stove were changed.

If we may speak of a third gardening stage of Aniceta's, thus balancing her exotic plantings, this one was utterly formal. Also in front of the house, a little way from the facade, behind a screen of oaks, she created a small Italian-style garden, which served to balance the bold exoticism of her botanical selections. This garden, of which there is no trace left today but which can be seen in old photographs, consisted of four lawns bordered by boxwood hedges and divided into four sections by a cross-shaped path. In the center an island bed was filled with colorful flowers, perhaps zinnias or pompon dahlias, another great favorite of Aniceta's. A parterre filled with various colored flowers, including an abundance of scarlet sage, was at each end of the great lawn in front of the villa. This was pruned by hand by a team of gardeners.

A number of lemon trees and orange trees, planted in elegant French-style containers of painted wood, were placed in both the front and back gardens of the villa. In order to satisfy this Mediterranean touch, a hothouse for lemon trees, which still exists, was built on the top terrace, below the church.

Aniceta was determined to continue transforming the land around the house into a magnificent garden of flower beds, fountains, exotic trees, and decorative statuary. Though her taste in gardens was unsophisticated, Aniceta justified her garden projects with energy and passion.

In 1890, her work in the garden was rewarded by the attention of the outside world. In a guidebook by the celebrated Gustavo Straffordello, published that year, we may read about the existence in Villar Perosa of "a magnificent palace surrounded by a grand and beautifully designed garden, which has been diligently decorated with a number of luxuriant paths bordered by leafy plants, citrus groves, and elaborate fountains."

In 1882, Giovanni finished junior high school. After more than ten years of widowhood, Aniceta had married Commendatore Luigi Lampugnani, a respected businessman with whom she would share a serene life.

The rustic bridge that Aniceta had built.

Marriage, however, did not distract her from the garden of Villar Perosa. Indeed, several displays of typical late-nineteenth-century and early-twentieth-century taste are to be found in other parts of the garden as well, signs of Aniceta's continual attention to the garden. A stone table and stone bench, their bases shaped like tree trunks with carved foliage, are still to be found today beneath the shade of a large magnolia tree on one of the terraces behind the villa. Here Aniceta and her second husband must have spent delightful hours sipping tea or perhaps even sometimes having breakfast served here during the summer months.

In addition, she had a long narrow bridge, made up of tree trunks and branches in the "rustic" style, built to unite the two ends of a small ravine, just east of the garden behind the villa. Beyond and a little below this ravine is the valley where, in the 1950s, Russell Page and Marella Agnelli created the lakes garden. Aniceta did not go as far as including this valley in her garden, but with this bridge and this ravine she undoubtedly added another dimension of spontaneous and wild nature to her increasingly eccentric garden.

Aniceta's old bridge, so paltry and out of tune with the architectural grace of the villa, was later redesigned by Russell Page in the Anglo-Chinese style that had been in vogue in the mid-eighteenth century. Certain features of Aniceta's passage through Villar Perosa were eliminated in the fifties and sixties in an attempt to give a more sober and unified appearance to the new park.

Other features, like her passion for exotic trees and for the fruit and vegetable gardens, as well as an overall rural quality that still characterizes the garden today, were actually enhanced.

The most fundamental aspect of Aniceta's passion, which survives in so many areas, is the way she was able to bring life to a relatively small eighteenth-century piece of land and transform it into something far more welcoming. Aniceta's garden was like a series of rooms, each very different from the other, in which both she and her family could spend pleasurable hours, according to the mood, season, or hour of the day. There was the arboretum in which to wander and wonder, the formal gardens, with their benches, in which to relax, the "natural" garden in which to take a walk, and many other spots in which to eat or read or simply admire the view of the mountains.

A few very old people in Villar Perosa still remember how, in the last years before her death, Aniceta loved to spend much of her time in the garden. One of her favorite spots in spring was a bench under a huge blossoming apple tree where the garden met the valley below. She would sit under this tree for hours at a time and knit or do petit point, an art that she very much enjoyed. Today the apple tree is still there, and from the wooden bench set against its trunk one can admire the lake garden and the mountains beyond.

The Senatore *and Clara: A Garden to Admire*

I don't think the senatore *and Clara, my grandparents, were particularly fond of gardening. For them, a garden was mainly a beautiful place to look at from the windows and that framed the villa. Every now and then, they would take a turn outside, around the fountain. Today, Villar has a marvelous garden, but at that time there wasn't much besides the great lawn in front and a small, Italian-style garden behind.*

—Susanna Agnelli, Porto Santo Stefano, Tuscany

For Giovanni Agnelli, who as an adult would be known by the title of *senatore,* Villar represented "the house of life" in every sense: belonging, deep affection, pride, and, when necessary, refuge. It was the house of life not only because he was born there, but because it was literally his house, having been inherited from his father when he was five years old. However, what made it special were his memories of happy summers and vacations spent there, in contrast with the frigid gray months of winter spent at the Collegio di San Giuseppe, in room 153.

How well he knew the surrounding valley: the clear Alpine sunsets, transparent when the sun disappeared behind the high hill of Assietta. Sitting in front of the villa at day's end, he and Aniceta would watch the sun fall, both of them tired—she from her gardening, and he from his excursions with the younger children of the farmers who helped his mother with her tasks. He knew the dawns glimpsed from the woods of Pramartino, when, hiding in secret with his playmates, he would climb the various larches, birches, and chestnut trees, from which he could spot the wide, rich Po plain washed in pink. From up high, he could imagine, more than see, Turin, so far away.

Behind him, though, the Villar Valley was still cloaked in the shadows of night. Below the mountains

Giovanni Agnelli in the uniform of an officer of the Third Savoy Cavalry, 1889.

lay the still sleeping silent farms, and beyond them the steeples of the bell towers of San Pietro in Vincoli, and still farther below, the villa's vast roof. In the villa itself, the *senatore* remembered the sounds of his own and his mother's footsteps echoing in the high stuccoed ceilings of the long gallery. Because he had so often gone with her and helped her, he knew every plant and blade of grass of the garden, of which in years to come he would be so proud and fond that he would want nothing changed. Although by nature innovative, the *senatore* was extremely conservative when it came to the garden of his childhood. He found Aniceta's accomplishments extraordinary and, with good reason, considered them somewhat his own. The increasingly numerous gardeners who came later were directed only to maintain the grounds, not change them. Thus, after Aniceta died, in 1920, the garden continued to mature. The old gardener, Gaetano Aloisio, allowed himself only a few variations on the basic design of the garden, and even this was only after World War II, with the excuse of removing the rubble from the villa's two bombed wings.

After boarding school, at his mother's suggestion, the young Giovanni Agnelli enrolled in the Accademia Militare di Cavalleria (the Cavalry Military Academy); in those years it was still considered the privileged and traditional path reserved for well-born young Piedmontesi. This choice, according to Valerio Castronuovo, one of Agnelli's principal biographers, was dictated in part by Aniceta's desire to see her social ambitions for her only son satisfied. It also gained him access to that narrow circle of relationships that was being formed at that time between the old aristocracy and the wealthy upper middle classes, especially the landowners, then coming to the fore.

In October 1884, Agnelli transferred to the strict and exclusive Accademia Militare in Modena, which he left, with officer's epaulets, two years later. He was promoted to lieutenant of the Third Savoy Cavalry in the spring of 1889, when he was twenty-three years old.

By then, he had already been married for a few months. In a letter from Verona dated August 23, 1888, to a fellow student at the academy, Carlo Policreti, Giovanni Agnelli announced his upcoming wedding:

I just arrived from Torino this morning. I have news for you that will surprise you very much—I am about to take a wife. I think that . . . in light of my previous conduct you would not predict that I would be a good husband, but they say that one changes that way after marriage. I would like to tell you also, speaking seriously, that I love her so much and have done so for so long that I have every reason to believe that we shall do very well together.

Here is the story. I have loved my cousin for five or six years, but because she is so serious, I never dared to give her the slightest hint of it. The other day I went to visit her in Levanto, at the beach resort, and I noticed, for the first time, that she was not indifferent to me. Finally I dared to declare myself. We were immediately engaged, but the nuptials will not take place until seven or eight months from now, which is why I pray you not to tell anyone.

I take this opportunity to thank you so very much for all the kindness I received at your home. Please thank your lady mother and your father and give my best regards to your brother.

Accept my condolences about the mare, poor beast! She was so sweet and ran so well. In any event I hope you will get over your mourning.

Farewell, dearest Carlo, I hope to see you soon at Villar, from where I will write you as soon as I arrive. In the meantime, here is an affectionate kiss from your very fond

—Agnelli

The date shows that Giovanni Agnelli had just turned twenty-two, but he writes of a love that he had had "for so long"—at least "five or six years." Clara would have been thirteen or fourteen years old and he himself a high-school student of sixteen or seventeen when it began. Clara Boselli and Giovanni Agnelli were married in Milan on February 2, 1889. He was twenty-two; she was not yet twenty. Theirs would be a powerful, blessed love story that would last for the rest of their lives.

It is likely that the two teenagers met at Aniceta and Luigi Lampugnani's wedding in 1882. Luigi's sister, Maddalena Lampugnani Boselli, had three girls and a boy from her marriage to Ingeniere Leopoldo Boselli. Clara was one of these children. So Luigi, who became Giovanni's stepfather, was Clara's uncle, and Aniceta became her aunt. The families surely met on more than one occasion, considering how close they were. Furthermore, the two brothers-in-law, Luigi Lampugnani and Leopoldo Boselli, were also good friends. They were both employed in the high ranks of the important new Ferrovie Mediterranee (Mediterranean Railroad). The railroad was important because transportation was essential to ensure the new nation's life. At the time, besides the modern railroad, there were only horse-drawn carriages. Commendatore Luigi Lampugnani was the chief director, while Leopoldo Boselli, Clara's father, was a well-respected engineer who, among other things, had designed and built the bold and complex Genoa–La Spezia stretch along the Ligurian coast.

Giovanni Agnelli and Clara Boselli at the time of their wedding, 1889.

Clara Boselli was born in Florence in 1870, but reared and educated in Milan. In the few pictures of her, she appears small next to her husband, who was taller than average. She was slender and held her tiny head high. She had very dark eyes in a face that would have been fashionable today, with its too large mouth and refined profile. These features emphasized her youthful appearance, from a childhood not entirely left behind. A rare photograph of Clara taken at the time shows us a pretty young woman whose fine, delicate features and refined style of dressing express an aura of appealing vulnerability. In time this vulnerability would lead her to choose a sheltered existence, taking refuge within the comforting confines of her own rooms. This reclusive tendency was to define, in later years, the lack of a relationship between her and the garden of Villar Perosa.

If it is true that opposites attract because of that mysterious something lacking in the other, Giovanni and Clara, with their successful union, were a striking example. It would be hard to imagine more different personalities.

Clara was not timid, but rather introverted. She wove her care and affections into deep and exclusive family ties. She did not enjoy, nor would she ever enjoy, life in society; she preferred to be alone. Simone de Beauvoir's phrase "L'ennui c'est les autres" could easily be applied to her. Above all, Clara enjoyed to read, and was equally facile in Italian and French. She would lose herself for hours on end in modern and contemporary literature—novels, short stories, and poems.

All her life Clara would display what was perhaps her only snobbishness: her enduring love of Parisian culture. She subscribed to some of the better-known literary magazines. Later, when she lived in Turin, she would have *Le Figaro* and *Le Temps* brought to her in the morning, along with the city dailies.

We don't know whether Clara was naturally retiring, or whether her aloofness was a reaction to Giovanni's boisterous nature.

Based on the descriptions by some of her grandchildren, she was both intelligent and cultured. Witty and light in conversation, she had an acutely observant nature that sometimes rendered her sharp or sarcastic. Giovanni and Clara both would retain throughout their life a vocabulary that was all their own, made up of intimacy and a certain humor that at times could become caustic.

Unlike his wife, Giovanni was stimulated by the outside world. He focused on resolving the countless complexities of day-to-day life; he was a man whose dreams turned into practical business goals and strategies.

Many of the written descriptions and anecdotes about Giovanni portray him as a man of extraordinary charisma, ironic sense of humor, and great intelligence. Carlo Biscaretti di Ruffia, one of Italy's automobile pioneers, first met Giovanni Agnelli in 1897. Many years later he wrote a short, affectionate account of this first meeting: "This man, a magnificent cavalry officer in civilian clothes [Agnelli had recently bade farewell to his military career], was of above-average height, robust, elegant, courteous. An imperious face, something powerful and sweet at the same time." The young Biscaretti di Ruffia also remarked how Agnelli could suddenly become very direct in his speech. "He had a reserved manner, but when he spoke the words came out curt, dry, explosive, as from a man born to command—biting and trenchant—and when one came to know him, ironic, even sarcastic. He also had a subtle sense of humor. Above all, a surprising frankness that at times left one breathless."

Years later, Giuseppe Bottai, minister of corporations between 1929 and 1932, would remember him thus: "One day they announced that Giovanni Agnelli is waiting outside. He comes in, greets me, sits down. He starts to talk to me, gets up, walks around, calls me 'young man,' talks for five minutes. I no longer knew if I was the minister or he was."

Married only a few months, and already wearing the silver epaulets of the Genoa Cavalry, Lieutenant Agnelli was transferred in the summer of 1889 to the Scuola di Applicazione (higher officers' training school) in Pinerolo. So he was once again very near Villar, if not actually there. It is very likely that Clara went to live there with her aunt Aniceta and uncle Luigi.

Aniceta had become very fond of her new daughter-in-law. Clara's fragility reminded her of one of the hothouse plants she so loved, needing protection and care. Clara also reminded her of Felicita, the daughter whom she had so wished to see grow up beside her, but who had died when still a baby. Probably, as with Giovanni, it was the differences between them that so appealed to Aniceta.

Clara loved to spend her days in the house, in the shelter of the loggias, with their thick walls, silence, and the dimly lit rooms where she often read. Aniceta, on the other hand, was happy only in the garden, in the open air. For her, housekeeping was nothing but duty, tedium, and annoyance. There were servants to urge on, to reprove, and meals to organize.

Clara, however, immediately demonstrated a delicate mastery of the daily rituals. With refined care, she could select the embroidered fine linen napkins from her trousseau, or the sets of dishes forgotten deep in some

Clara Boselli Agnelli during the first years of her marriage.

cupboard, or the cut-crystal pitchers for fruit juice. The staff came to love her—she paid attention to their work, something Aniceta had always done as little as possible and grudgingly, because she preferred to chase after some new gardening strategy. And Clara loved Aniceta, too, if only for the great affection that Aniceta showed her. She was learning, however, in those first days at Villar the subtle and complex art of gaining the affection of the people closest to her. It was an art in which she would show herself a master in the years to come.

In August 1891, Giovanni Agnelli was transferred to Verona. Clara and Giovanni introduced themselves to society by moving into the ancient Palazzo Balladore. But his new life, shuttling between the garrison and his duties, must have seemed infinitely monotonous to Giovanni, and the prospect of it extending over a long career, unbearable. In addition, both Clara and Giovanni had difficulty tolerating the many ceremonies and social obligations that military life required. Already in 1892 he requested a leave of absence, then later took a final retirement from military service, effective July 17, 1893. This apparently inexplicable whim evoked Aniceta's most implacable disapproval. She tried everything to change his mind. She even attempted to convince her daughter-in-law to threaten divorce unless Giovanni changed his mind, but to no avail. This must have been a difficult period for Aniceta, as she was forced to relinquish the dreams of military leadership and glory that she had had for Giovanni.

In the summer of 1892, when he was twenty-six years old, Giovanni returned to Villar Perosa with his wife and their two young children, Aniceta (better known as Tina) and Edoardo. Within a brief time, he took in hand the administration of the agricultural holdings established by Giuseppe Francesco, and subsequently run so well by his father, then so assiduously by Aniceta. The principal crop was still, as in his grandfather's day, mulberry trees on which the silkworms fed. But a series of hindrances and natural calamities that struck the silk producers of Piedmont—such as a recurring and devastating disease among the worms, followed by a customs war with France that abruptly interrupted the distribution channels for Italian silk—persuaded Giovanni Agnelli to review the crops under cultivation. By raising and selling livestock, forage, and wood, he managed to keep intact, if not increase, much of the family patrimony.

In order to invest further, he drew up a contract of surety dated May 27, 1897, and executed to protect Clara, using Villar Perosa as collateral for a part of her dowry (100,000 lire at that time). This agreement turns out to be an interesting source of information on the state of the property and garden as they were at the end of the last century: "This great piece of land is made up of the Castle, the former fief of the Counts of Perosa, with quite a large English garden, tower, and hothouse, all modernized, elegantly kept and walled in . . . buildings, farms . . . vegetable gardens, fields, mulberry trees, grapevines, woods, river meadows, and pastures."

Now he owned everything worth owning in Villar and environs; nor was the situation such as to allow him to invest his money any other way. In the long run, his part in local government and his management of his family's estate had not succeeded in allowing him to don the role of country gentleman, of a provincial personage.

—Valerio Castronuovo, *Agnelli*

Now Giovanni did what he had done in Verona. He decided to go further and explore new and exciting shores: Turin and the new industrial age.

In the last decade of the nineteenth century, Turin had become an active metropolis that managed to combine old-world values with the cultural dynamism of a modern city. Friedrich Nietzsche, who had spent time in Turin between 1888 and 1889, described it as a "peaceful, almost solemn city." He added, however, that Turinese evenings offered many entertainments, such as the theater, ballrooms, and the popular *cafés chantants,* or cabarets.

In the wake of the crises of the preceding years, Turin was finally finding its true identity as a modern and industrial city. Edmondo De Amicis, a popular Italian author of the nineteenth century, described Turin in the 1880s as a city in perpetual motion.

Everybody walks looking straight ahead; people talk without slowing their pace; loud conversations are rare. . . . And in the busiest streets one can see, as in the great northern cities, a sort of race to arrive first, to leave behind the people walking beside us, as if every neighbor were a business rival. . . . However, a certain appearance of civility makes up for the somewhat harsh quality of that rushed lifestyle of an industrial city.

Aesthetically, Turin had all the cheerful exuberance of a modern city and looked like one. Tramways crammed with people brightened the evening darkness with their moving lights. Restaurants and shops opened their doors along the streets and in the increasingly crowded squares, while the outskirts were growing at a fast pace as more and more people migrated into town from the countryside looking for jobs in the many factories. Out of a population of about 300,000 people, more than one-quarter worked in the manufacturing sector.

The "auto-mobile" vehicle is the great fin-de-siècle novelty. In Turin, about one hundred of them are already in circulation, still eyed by passersby with curiosity mixed with suspicion. All, or almost all, are driven at the hour when people take the air, along Corso Vittorio, amid the carriages, berlins, landaus, and coupés of the aristocracy and wealthy upper middle classes. And since Caffè Burello, on the corner of the Corso and Via Rattazzi, was the place where the carriages slowed down to allow the ladies carried in them to see and be seen, the rattling automobiles and their crews formed the habit of stopping in the same way and in the same place.

These, too, like Turin's beautiful women, were placed on display, to be admired by the motley audience that met there: aristocrats and bourgeois, idlers and travelers from the nearby train station of Porta Nuova, who sat on red velvet armchairs and sofas, exchanging news and gossip about business, politics, women, and money, and holding forth, often very animatedly, on everything and everybody.

The roar of the motors, which soon became familiar at the corner of Corso Vittorio, ended up making the Burello the place where the automobile fanatics met, and, among the most regular, a group of friends whose discussions on the subject revealed something more than a disinterested passion.

—Angiolo Silvio Ori, *Storia di una Dinastia: Gli Agnelli e la Fiat*

Giovanni Agnelli was one of these.

So it was that on July 1, 1899, four years before Henry Ford founded his company in Dearborn, Michigan, the cavalry officer became a partner in a new firm, the Società per la Costruzione ed il Commercio delle

Plan of the "Agnelli Farmstead," a gift to the senatore *on the occasion of a bicycle rally, August 27, 1904.*

Automobili Torino, whose name was almost immediately changed to Fabbrica Italiana Automobili Torino, or Fiat. It marked the birth of the Fiat empire.

The great boost to the Italian automobile industry occurred a few years later, after Agnelli's merger with R.I.V., the first Italian ball-bearing manufacturer. Before then, these little steel spheres used in internal-combustion engines were imported at prohibitive cost from other countries, in particular Sweden and Germany. After the merger, R.I.V. would be located in the heart of the Val Chisone, hard by the village of Villar Perosa. It was inaugurated in 1906. At that time, the success of Fiat, which was already producing some 1,200 cars a year, was surpassing every expectation. The factory in Corso Dante, in Turin, was expanding every year, and the stock market prices, quoted at 900 lire in 1905, shot up to 1,900 lire in the summer of 1906.

It took another five or six years of growth before Giovanni and Clara Agnelli ceased to manage the property of Villar Perosa as if it were the family's chief source of income. Now, on the contrary, they saw its value as a magnificent symbol of their new economic and social status.

A hand-painted map of the entire Agnelli property, which was presented to Giovanni Agnelli in 1904 as a gift in memory of a bicycle race across part of his property, shows a garden whose size had remained virtually unchanged for many years. It is relatively small and hemmed in by fields under cultivation, mostly fruit trees, planted wherever possible here and there to take advantage of good soil. A guidebook to Italian castles and villas, published in 1911, describes the garden of Villa Agnelli as a romantic setting in which "pleasant lawns" alternated delightfully with "small woods of ancient trees." This brief description suggests that in 1911 the garden was still aesthetically rooted in Aniceta's nineteenth-century sensibility.

In that same year, great changes were begun in the villa itself. In a 1912 publication by Giovanni Chevalley, *Gli architetti, l'architettura e la decorazione delle ville piemontesi del XVIII secolo,* we learn that

> *The Agnelli family, the present owners, have recently undertaken significant restorations and improvements under the supervision of Count Carlo Ceppi and the collaboration of Ingeniere [engineer] Carlo Nasi.*
>
> *What is most noteworthy in this villa is the variously colored stuccowork in the very fine gallery and in the chapel, and that decorating the ceilings in certain areas; the double-ramped grand stairway and the facade recall in places the grand stairway and the facade of Palazzo Madama, designed in Turin by Juvarra.*

Now Giovanni Agnelli wanted to install every modern comfort in his home. Except for the main drawing room in the middle, the suite of public rooms on the second floor was turned into bedrooms, each with its own large bathroom. To this end, much of the outside, east-facing loggia at the back of the house was closed off. In this way, Giovanni arranged things so that the most beautiful grand room of the house became Clara's bedroom, as he knew her fondness for spending many hours there every day. This room must have been considered the most important one even in the planning stage given its privileged southern exposure, the magnificent stuccowork and the fireplace, and the genuine *papier de Chine* (Chinese wallpaper) that covered it all. Giovanni also had a balcony built for Clara from which she could look at the garden and listen to the rushing of a little torrent of deliciously cold water at the bottom of the valley.

In 1905, Aniceta was again widowed and so came to live at Villar Perosa, where a suite was made for her. An elevator, extraordinary in a country house of the time, was installed to take Aniceta to her rooms. Meanwhile, the great kitchens were entirely renovated, as were the stables, which were turned into modern "garages."

A few short lines published in the local newspaper, *L'Eco del Chisone,* on August 17, 1912, announced the arrival of the family at Villar Perosa. "The Agnelli family has finally arrived among us. Because of some construction under way in their magnificent residence, this year the generous family was obliged to delay their arrival among us and the benefits of breathing our health-giving mountain air."

Soon after, *senatore* Agnelli announced his intention to sponsor the badly needed restoration of the Church of San Pietro in Vincoli. This public act of generosity would be followed by others: the creation of schools, old-age homes, churches, and hospitals, as well as the two large, modern sanitariums of Pra Catinat.

In 1921, the year after Aniceta died, Giacomo Grosso painted a detailed view of the garden east of the villa. It shows a large square lawn, with a simple fountain in the classical style at its center, framed by a number of flower borders and smaller rectangular lawns. Narrow gravel paths lead the way through this part of the garden. Citrus trees placed in pots stand at each side of the wide round arches that support the villa's upper loggia.

A description of Villar in a contemporary guidebook to Pinerolo and environs, published in 1922, completes the picture. The villa, one reads, is surrounded by gardens of a rare beauty, "in which one finds luxuriant growth of various types of citrus trees, cedars of Lebanon, rose apple trees and rare shrubs and flowers. Fountains, jets, and spurts complete the beauty of this sumptuous castle."

All in all, it seems, the Agnelli garden had gradually become full of delicate sounds, scents, and colors that could be admired and enjoyed from the quiet of one's own rooms or, as Clara liked to do, from the balcony.

Clara and the *senatore*'s children, Tina and Edoardo, had married young, and by the mid-1920s the family was much larger. Born in 1921, Gianni Agnelli, the son of Edoardo and his wife, Virginia, remembers the summers spent at Villar Perosa with his many siblings and cousins as a particularly happy period of his early childhood. "Villar was a very important part of our childhood," he says today, "because we would go there at the end of every summer, for the month of September. We were so many, eleven or twelve children."

Avvocato Agnelli also remembers that there was a great separation in the main house, at that time, between the lives led by the children and those of the adults:

> The life of the family was regulated by a great sense of discipline. There were the governesses who took care of us. By the late twenties we were already so many brothers and sisters that the villa's top floor was set aside for us. We could get to our parents' rooms on the floor below by elevator, and since we were forbidden to ride in it we enjoyed it.
>
> There was also a vast terrace, with red geraniums, from where you can still see the bell towers of San Pietro in Vincoli, but even more, hear the carillon that Grandfather had had installed and that could be heard throughout the village.
>
> Our Nasi cousins, who were also many, stayed in the children's cottage. There was discipline, but there was also some time to play. We would play tennis at the far end of the garden. We were allowed to spend a lot of time on our own, but we were expected to be on time for meals.

Respect for schedules and customs was the basis of daily life for the many children at Villar Perosa. There was a time for eating and a time for taking a walk or playing, another for studying or simply for sitting together and chatting and admiring the scenery. Every moment of the day was part of a greater plan with consideration of how time should be spent effectively. Even the timing of visits to Villar Perosa was carefully regulated. "My grandparents," explains Countess Maria Sole Agnelli Teodorani, younger sister of Gianni, "would arrive at

The senatore *with his wife, Clara, and the families of Edoardo and Virginia*
Agnelli and of Carlo and Tina Nasi, at Villar Perosa around 1924.

Villar at the beginning of September and stay until the day of Saint Edward, October 13. I remember they liked to fix the dates of their trips far in advance." The earlier part of the summer was normally spent at a villa that the Agnellis had in Levanto, in Liguria. During the summer the *senatore* often went on short cruises. Clara, on the other hand, went to stay in the mountains, at the Hotel Suvretta in Saint Moritz, Switzerland.

When in Villar, the *senatore* would wake up early in the morning and go down to the garden for breakfast and to read his paper sitting at a small wicker table in the shade of an awning over the main entrance. At exactly 7:30, after looking in on his grandchildren having their breakfast, he went back upstairs to say good morning to Clara, then took off by car for his office in Turin.

The *senatore* reappeared every evening around seven in time to walk with Clara, who loved that time of day. Their customary walk was almost invariably the same: around the fountain. These recollections are based on the observations made by Agostino Stella, the elderly butler.

By the time the *senatore* returned, the younger children would already have had dinner in the small dining room in the Nasi wing that was reserved for them. If they lingered too long, they would without fail be admonished to hurry up and finish. Ready for the night in their colorful little dressing gowns, they were sent to bed together with their nursemaids as soon as possible by Agostino himself, who wanted to see to his preparations for the evening free of other worries. But the children who were a little older were allowed to eat in the large dining room with their parents, grandparents, aunts and uncles, and the occasional guest. "In the evening," recalls Clara Agnelli Nuvoletti, the eldest daughter of Edoardo and Virginia, "we changed clothes but did not get dressed up." This is to indicate that it continued to be a family setting in a bourgeois atmosphere, even though it was very formal.

The other men would put on dark suits, just as the *senatore* unfailingly did. The ladies would wear simple dresses of light silk in clear colors, because the summer had not yet come to an end. If it had gotten cooler following an end-of-the-season thunderstorm or a sudden wind from the nearby mountains, they would bring out their light woolen shawls or capotes; Clara, however, always wore some sort of covering.

Maria Sole recalls that after meticulous preparations, her grandmother would come downstairs from her rooms trailing a faint but recognizable scent of cologne and verbena. Her mother, Virginia, would have sprayed her scarves and the back of her hair with one of the strong French perfumes, such as L'heure bleue by Guerlain, which were already fashionable and which her mother-in-law considered to be in *mauvais ton* (bad taste).

Also in the way she dressed, Clara rejected what was new, especially in the evening. She would always remain faithful to the guipures of handmade lace that framed her face with its long row of little buttons along the sides. After Mina, her personal maid, had fastened those countless little buttons, she would attach a pearl clasp onto the soft laces. Aside from Clara's guipures, which were somewhat unusual, the other ladies intentionally dressed in a simple manner. But the table that was set for them was far from simple, according to Agostino Stella's detailed description of it to Marella Agnelli. Clara supervised every detail of the household meticulously and with great care. But she lavished particular attention on those times of the day—and the year—when all the people she loved were gathered under that same roof.

From the big dining room on the ground floor one could see the fountain and Aniceta's well-tended, colorful parterres through the large windows. The view was the same as the one in the 1921 painting by Grosso. The middle of the room was taken up by a large oval table, on which the tablecloths were changed every day. It meant a lot to Clara if someone noticed their variety. They alternated between the ones made of linen, which she had had embroidered in certain convents or in Florence, and those made of heavy Flanders flax whose napkins, decorated in the corners with the "A" of the house, were so big that they seemed to be bedsheets.

Agnese Basso Aloisio, the wife of the gardener Gaetano Aloisio, supervised the laundry. After she received instructions from Clara, she would have lengthy discussions with her husband in order to choose the flowers that would best suit the tablecloths. Agostino, in his capacity as butler, would get involved on the rebound with regard to the china and the centerpieces for the table. These flowers for the table were perhaps the only interest that Clara took in the garden.

Everything was comfortable, well tended, and refined, but the Villar household of that time had basically remained bourgeois. The enormous growth of Fiat and the ensuing power of the *senatore* had in no way changed Clara's and Giovanni's domestic habits, which remained intentionally the same, quiet and without showiness. Was there any luxury? Hardly. They preferred comfort without ostentatiousness. There were no outward signs that mirrored the sensational industrial success, the economic power, or the influence on politics that is never far removed from big business.

"Every Sunday," Gianni Agnelli explains, "my grandfather went to Villar Perosa to perform his duties as mayor." Despite his love of the mountains, the woods, and nature in general, the *senatore* had little free time to take long walks. At the most, you could see him from time to time on Saturdays or Sundays, with his pipe between his teeth, climbing the steep path that he knew from his childhood and which led to the hill of the Pramartino woods, which overlooks both the town and the villa. At other times, he would only accompany his wife during her short daily excursions in the garden.

Clara's days at Villar, like those of her husband, began very early in the morning. "The first thing Grandmother would do," relates Umberto Nasi, "was call the maids. Mina, her personal maid, would then brush her hair at length while she sat in front of her 'coiffeuse' dressing table. Together with Maria Candida and Maria Bianca, the two sisters who helped her with the laundry, Agnese would meanwhile change the pillowcases on Clara's bed and tidy up the entire room. Once Clara had completed her toilet, which was always meticulous, she would have been helped, generally by Mina, into one of those divine 'robes d'intérieur' (exquisite house dresses) with a gauzy collar of embroidered tulle.

"Now she was perfect," Umberto Nasi added. "And, completely ready, she would wait for Grandfather to come and say good-bye before he left for Turin and the tasks of the day."

The relationship between the *senatore,* who was so active and involved with his work, and his wife, who preferred a secluded life, was intimate and affectionate. The *senatore* was extremely attached to his wife, and many people say he was even devoted to her. Although Clara always led a very retiring life, she had considerable influence not only on her husband but also on her children—and, consequently, on their families as well.

Once the sound of the car engine on the access road faded into the distance, Clara would return to bed or stretch out on the big wicker lounging chair that she had ordered to be placed in the gallery. There she would spend the remainder of the morning or the entire day, depending on how she felt, on her mood, on the interest she had in what she was reading, or on how much she wanted the company of the guests who were then in the house. In the silence of those long hours of isolation in her rooms, she would nurture the need for solitude and absolute tranquillity that was the precursor of her much-sought-after interior peace.

A large wooden serving wagon, as Agostino described it, equipped with rubber wheels, would be pushed next to the bed and sometimes into the gallery near the lounging chair or even, if needed, out onto the balcony. On its shelves were books of current interest, literary magazines, and French fashion magazines. Clara was elegant. The seamstress Prieri, who was considered the best in Turin, would come to visit at her Via Giacosa address when Clara was in the city. The seamstress would bring her other Parisian magazines, and they would endlessly compare to Italian clothes, or discuss various swatches of material. It was all just "talk," for Clara dressed strictly in white, black, or pearl gray.

"I would have given anything while I was an adolescent to have a dress made by the seamstress Prieri," relates Maria Sole Agnelli Teodorani, who had admired the cut and the work done by Prieri in dresses belonging to both her mother, Virginia, and her older sister Clara.

Clara loved Paris. Whenever she spent a few days there together with the *senatore,* she came to life and went to the opera, the theater, and the museums. But she never bought herself a dress designed by one of the great fashion houses of the French capital. In this, she was very different from Virginia, who had a predilection for the Paris designer Vionnet as well as the seamstress Prieri. Only for the wedding of her favorite granddaughter, Clara Agnelli, did she order a three-quarter-length coat of sable. "She thought that a cloak was too extravagant," Clara Agnelli Nuvoletti adds.

At Villar, however she spent her day, in the evening she would come downstairs without fail. She did this not only because she liked to take her ritual walk with Giovanni after he came home, but also because she would wait with trepidation for the return home of Edoardo, her much-loved son.

Edoardo, too, was extremely attached to his mother. "My father adored her," explains Suni Agnelli. "He went to visit her almost every day of his life. I believe that she was an intelligent and well-educated woman, because my father, who was a man who used to read literature and who enjoyed reading, did not just love her very much but enjoyed conversing with her." "They had the same sense of humor," adds Clara Agnelli Nuvoletti, "and they would laugh together about the same things."

From the beginning of the twenties until World War II, the mood at Villar Perosa was marked by conflicting events. During that time, and increasingly with each summer, Villar took on the inviting and "lived-in" look of a grandparents' home. The twelve grandchildren of the *senatore* and Clara (Umberto, the youngest of the children of Edoardo and Virginia Agnelli, was born in 1934) filled the children's wings and the garden with their young voices, their games, and their governesses. Numerous photographs show the Agnelli children and their Nasi cousins in bright little pedal-cars in front of the villa, playing in a wooden cart, or in a group together with their parents, their grandparents, and a few dogs. These images, taken in the garden during summer vacations at Villar Perosa, evoke the happy and carefree atmosphere of a large family. But the premature death of Tina Agnelli Nasi in 1928 and the death of her brother, Edoardo, barely seven years later would leave a painful void in the lives of Clara and the *senatore* as well as, inevitably, in the childhood memories of their children.

Tina Agnelli Nasi (Aniceta was her real name; she had been named after her grandmother) had married Carlo Nasi in 1912, but had remained very attached to her parents, her mother in particular. Even after the birth of her children, Tina continued to spend the last part of summer every year with her parents at Villar Perosa. The so-called children's wing next to the villa was constructed at the wish of the *senatore* for Tina's chil-

Virginia Bourbon del Monte, circa 1920s.

dren; it was designed by Count Carlo Ceppi with the help of Carlo Nasi, an engineer and talented architect who had also drawn the plans for the Levanto villa. Tina suddenly died on May 21, 1928, shortly after the birth of their fifth child, Emanuele. Suni Agnelli, who was only six or seven years old when her aunt died, recalled in her memoirs the mood that prevailed at home after Tina's death: "The only thing I remember about her death is a great confusion at home and crowds of people who kept going in and out of all the rooms. I heard people saying that my grandmother was distraught." Suni's father, Edoardo Agnelli, died on a warm summer day in July 1935 in an airplane accident, shortly after landing in a hydroplane off the shores of Genoa.

Photographs of Edoardo show a handsome man whose finely chiseled features and elegant way of dressing remind us of the physiognomy and the style of his mother Clara. His physical characteristics were the same as those that would be typical of many members of the Agnelli family for the next two or more generations. These included a high, broad forehead, almond-shaped eyes that were slightly bulging, and finely drawn lips curving into an ironic and attractive smile. Like his father, Edoardo received a spartan education. During World War I, he was sent to the high command at Udine as a cavalry officer in the reserves, in order to serve as deputy director of the automotive center. His experience in the military did not diminish his passion for reading and a social life. These interests were perhaps fostered by a rather delicate physical constitution. "He is really consumptive," wrote the author and journalist Ugo Ojetti in a letter to his wife. "I went by myself to have tea with Mrs. Clara Agnelli. She became emotional when she talked about Edoardo, who seems to have been in very serious condition last winter."

Edoardo Agnelli, circa 1920s.

This physical weakness, heightened by Clara's ever-present anxiety, was partly responsible for the fact that Edoardo always felt intimidated by his father, who was so charismatic and successful. In his efforts to find a part of his own to play, Edoardo began to devote himself to transforming his passion for sports into a business. As president of Juventus, the young Agnelli succeeded in putting this Turinese soccer team on the road to success. Under his direction, it took the team only a few years to reach a pinnacle of success that continues to this day. He understood, long before many others did, what an extraordinary hold soccer had on a large part of the population, and he sensed its potential as an image and a commercial venture. Edoardo Agnelli was the first person in Italy to buy good foreign players for high prices and then treat them as real celebrities. He offered them beautiful homes, cars with drivers, and salaries that, at the time, were considered exorbitant. His insight proved to be valid once more when, in 1932, he devoted himself to the very successful founding of one of the most futuristic and attractive ski resorts in Europe. This was Sestriere, to the north of the Chisone Valley.

Going to the mountains to await the return of spring is fashionable. Sestriere is an out-of-the-way hill located between the Chisone Valley and the Susa Valley among steep, bare mountains. Edoardo Agnelli has a good eye, and clever advisers, which enabled him to come to the conclusion that there is nothing better than this location for building a big ski center. It is only a few kilometers from the train station of Oulx, a few hours by car from Turin, in the middle of a dense network of very interesting ski courses at high altitudes. The big yellow towers are erected; the cables of the cableway are

Virginia Agnelli with her children, from left to right, Gianni, Clara, Suni,
Maria Sole, Cristiana (in Virginia's arms), at Forte dei Marmi, 1927.

put in place; a large clientele gathers immediately. Sestriere made an impression and constituted
the beginning of an era in Europe. It was an important turning point and a big business deal in
the world of skiing, which moved rapidly from sealskins to the cable car ticket.

—Italo Pietra, *The Three Agnelli, Giovanni, Edoardo, Gianni*

Edoardo was barely thirty years old when Mussolini came to power in 1922. Despite the ambivalent feelings that the *senatore* had for il Duce, Edoardo was attracted by the apparent youthful dynamism of the Fascist Party—or perhaps he was again looking for an image and a role that would allow him to differentiate himself from the commanding personality of his father. On the other hand, many members of the party saw in him the young entrepreneur and probable successor to the *senatore,* one of the important personalities of the new generations. Despite his increasing public role, the young Edoardo had continued to patronize the fashionable salons and the beautiful and aristocratic women who enlivened them. One of these, Virginia Bourbon del Monte, a very young woman, became his wife.

The aristocratic world of papal ties, from which Virginia came, and her anticonformist and sociable nature, which she inherited from her American mother, were in marked contrast to the sober and reserved atmosphere that prevailed in the Agnelli household. Her father, Carlo Bourbon del Monte, descended from a family of ancient nobility. The Bourbon del Montes had for many centuries exercised control over a large part of the territories of Tuscany and Umbria that bordered on the Papal States. Around 1870, Pope Pius IX finally

*From left to right: Clara, Gianni (at the wheel), Cristiana,
Giorgio, Suni, Maria Sole, early 1930s. Photo, Bricarelli*

granted them the title of princes of San Faustino. Carlo Bourbon del Monte avoided the use of that title, which

he considered too new and devoid of meaning in comparison with the ancient marquessate to which he belonged

and which had its roots in history. His American wife, however, valued the title of prince and used it without

hesitation. Virginia's mother, Jane Allen Campbell, whose friends and relatives affectionately called her Princess

Jane for this reason, was an eccentric American woman known by many for her sense of humor, her sharp wit

and intelligence, and her bons mots. Most of all, however, she was known for her love of acting as hostess and

being hosted herself. Virginia Bourbon del Monte, who was young (barely twenty years old when she married

Edoardo in 1919), beautiful, and both totally natural and sophisticated at the same time, represented a breath

of fresh air that shook up not only the somewhat reserved and bourgeois world of Turin of those years but also

the Agnelli family itself. "She loved life and fun," Susanna Agnelli wrote years later when she described her

mother in her memoirs. "She was totally uneducated, she made incredible spelling mistakes when writing in

Italian, she was madly generous both with friends and with strangers. She remained always and in essence a

young girl."

Apart from some beautiful pictures and the memories of those who had a chance to get to know her,

there are not many documents that help to evoke Virginia Agnelli's personality. Other than her beauty and her

love of life, the principal character trait that clearly appears in the various memories and anecdotes that portray

her is the way in which she was able to attract the attention and devotion of those who met her. Children as much

as adults were drawn to her by her straightforward ways and her vitality. The people of the town of Villar Perosa who knew her remember her with affection. One of the most evocative written descriptions of Virginia was found in an unpublished diary written by Vittorio Bonadé Bottino, head of what was then the construction department of Fiat. In these unpublished pages, the engineer describes a lunch with Edoardo and Virginia at Villar Perosa that took place in the beginning of the thirties.

> *Edoardo Agnelli liked to stay at the villa during the spring and fall. He ran into me one morning in the factory and invited me to lunch, where he introduced me to his wife, Virginia Bourbon del Monte. She is young, tall, slender despite having already had five children, extremely vivacious, almost restless, truly courteous, and so charming as to dispel the sense of awe experienced at one's first encounter with a lady known as the First Lady of Turin. And this not only because of her name and family background, but also because her elegance, her manners, and her animated vitality are such as to naturally place her in a category of rare distinction.*
>
> *In the early afternoon of that same day, Donna Virginia took the wheel of a two-seater Balilla and, with me seated next to her, she drove me to the Sanatoriums at Pra Catinat. The trip, made at high speed over the road of the Assietta mountain, which was open to the traffic of trucks headed for the building yard . . . , did not lack for occasions when the car would start sliding in the curves, at which times the undaunted driver would respond by laughing merrily. Very satisfied with the visit, she then sent me off wishing me similar success with the work for the first facility at the Sestriere mountain during the coming two months.*

Edoardo and Virginia lived their short lives together at an accelerated, often frenetic, pace. Not even the births of seven children, all between 1920 and 1934, could persuade them to live a calmer and more traditional life.

When they were in Turin during the winter, they were an integral part of the social life of the city's elite. At that time, the prince and princess of Piedmont were still living in Turin with their court, and the Royal Palace was often used for grand receptions. Edoardo and Virginia participated in the life of the court. Virginia was very active in this even though she was too much of a free spirit to submit herself completely to the rigors of court life. In her memoirs, Susanna Agnelli provides a detailed description of the preparations that were made for one of the dinners given by Virginia and Edoardo Agnelli for the prince and princess of Piedmont.

> *Some evenings, a great nervousness prevails among the servants. One of them walks all through the house, through the library and the living rooms, up and down the marble staircase, holding an iron coal-shovel filled with burning embers. Every ten steps he pauses and, from a bottle he holds in his other hand, he pours an oily liquid on the burning embers. The scented vapors slide up and around*

the curtains, the tapestries, the paintings, and remain in the air. Vigiassa (one of the maids) tells me that the Prince of Piedmont is coming to dinner and that "Mamma" has given instructions that we should be ready and waiting, all dressed the same way, in the downstairs entranceway to make our curtsies when the Prince and Princess arrive. Daddy and Mommy stand next to us at the feet of the staircase. Gianni is in his sailor suit while we four sisters are wearing dresses embroidered with tiny roses. My father is nervous because, as usual, my mother was not ready at the time he had set. My mother looks very beautiful. Under the portico, the headlights of a car appear. The heavy glass door is opened wide by Guglielmo, who looks more handsome and important than ever in his dark blue livery. The Prince and Princess enter. They are real Royals. He is in uniform and he is smiling. She is wearing a diamond tiara and her blue eyes are dreamy. They are both young, handsome, and happy. We make our bows and they kiss us on the hair. Then they start going up the staircase and we are sent off to bed.

"Fast cars, gambling, beautiful women"—this stereotype of the period could very well have been used to describe Edoardo's inclinations. But the worldly consequences of his Gatsby-type life must not have been to the liking of the *senatore.* In order to keep him closer to himself and to provide him with interests that would be more in line with the responsibilities that awaited him, as well as to please Clara and satisfy her ambitions for her son, the *senatore* had Edoardo appointed to innumerable positions. His titles are too vast to list here, but those that stand out include member of the Board of Directors of IFI, vice president of Fiat, and former president of the Società Anomime Officine di Villar Perosa, R.I.V.

It was during one of these changes from one position to another that Edoardo died, at the age of only forty-four, in a plane crash in the harbor at Genoa.

Newspaper articles published over the following days described the event as a great loss that had befallen not only the family but also the whole nation. In the July 15 edition of *La Gazzetta del Popolo della Sera,* one can read how thousands upon thousands of people, including politicians, members of Parliament, industrialists, scientists, public officials, artists, and many other personalities went to extend their condolences to the Agnelli family. Even more people participated in the funeral cortege that took place in Turin. Judging from the newspapers of the time, the cortege took on the proportions of a state funeral. In *La Nuova Stampa* on July 17, there is a long article describing in detail "an impressive demonstration of grief on the part of the populace," in which "an entire city wept for a man." Thousands of Fiat workers participated in the procession. Virginia was too much in shock to take part in the procession; Clara did not even attend the funeral. After the funeral, the body was taken to Villar Perosa for burial.

The following weeks were spent in mourning at Villar Perosa, we are told by Giuseppe Gabrielli, a famous aircraft designer who was a friend of the family and the author of a biography entitled *Una Vita per l'Aviazione*.

> *This disaster had an enormous effect on all of Italy and in particular at Fiat. The dignity and strength of character displayed by* senatore *Agnelli were exceptional. Once he had arrived at the cemetery of Villar, the* senatore *stood near the entrance in order to follow the sad ceremony from afar. He stood straight, without moving, and his eyes remained dry and staring fixedly. He stood in this manner until the end, while leaning with one arm on my shoulder. It is easy to imagine the speculation during those days. People asked themselves, "Will the* senatore *return to Fiat?" while the usual so-called well-informed people said that Agnelli would abandon the company.*

Gabrielli adds, "Days went by, but the *senatore* did not show up." Then, one September morning, he appeared at an important meeting together with Vittorio Valletta. "Agnelli looked at us as if to greet us and thank us at the same time," Gabrielli writes. "He then sat down in his usual place and said in a strong voice, 'I am here to continue what my son should have done.'

"He put on his glasses, quickly glanced at the agenda that he had in front of him and opened the meeting with, 'So the last time we had gotten to. . . .'"

The *senatore* dealt with his great sorrow by immersing himself even more in his work and in the activities of the company. He also began to pay closer attention to the educational development of Gianni, his favorite grandchild, for whom he now experienced that feeling of continuity he had lost with the sudden death of Edoardo. Clara, however, could no longer find the strength to react. She hardly ever left her rooms anymore and spent long hours in solitude. But she could no longer find the serenity of times past and she sank into a bottomless melancholy.

All that summer of 1935, Villar Perosa was a place of mourning. The grandchildren remained with their grandparents until the opening of the schools in October. As Umberto Nasi recalled, "The generation in between, that is to say the generation of my parents and of Virginia and Edoardo, lived a short life. . . . They all died before the *senatore* and his wife. . . . It is difficult to imagine how their presence would have influenced the evolution of Villar Perosa and its garden."

During the years that followed, the habits in the old dwelling continued to be repeated. Giovanni and Clara would open the house as usual during the first days of September and stay until mid-October. And, as usual, the grandchildren were with them.

From then on, the garden was left completely in the care of the gardener, Gaetano Aloisio. With the help of some assistant gardeners, Gaetano would mow the lawns, prune the roses, trim the hedges, and rake the gravel paths every morning, removing every leaf and every imprint and keeping the garden in perfect condition.

From the protected silence of her rooms, or from the balcony, Clara would check that everything was carried out meticulously and that, at least in the garden, nothing should change. Villar Perosa had to remain an oasis apparently untouched by the events of reality. Peace and quiet were precious in Clara's garden and strident, uncontrolled noises were not allowed. Likewise, the smaller children were forbidden to run or play noisily under her windows or climb in the trees that surrounded the villa. These years before World War II were a hiatus in the history of the gardens of Villar Perosa. And, despite the impetuous presence of so many grandchildren, everything was maintained in accordance with a code of repetitive order that could guarantee Clara, in her sorrowful withdrawal, the peace and quiet that she needed more and more.

Every morning, when she awoke, Clara would sit on her bed waiting for the comforting sound of the metal rake on the gravel of the path under her windows. And then she would call Mina.

After 1940 and Italy's entry into the war, the family lived through a period of separation. Villar Perosa remained shut for some time. But in 1942, the *senatore* and his wife decided to take refuge there. During this period, which was also marked by political and social tensions and by numerous strikes even within the company, Villar—with its tended garden, its gurgling fountains, its shady lanes, and the loyal presence of the old servants—must have seemed a last refuge to the *senatore* and Clara, an oasis of peace and serenity in a world that was ever more insecure and stormy. This peace, however, did not last long.

There was great fear in the valley that the Allied forces would choose the R.I.V as a strategic objective for possible bombardment. The *senatore* had the factory and the church painted a coppery green color in the hope of camouflaging them. He did not do the same for the villa, feeling certain that it would not be a target. But he was wrong. On January 3, 1944, around noon, a deafening whistling sound announced that bombs were falling in the area. There followed perhaps two or three minutes of hell, during which buildings were destroyed, trees were uprooted, and an enormous cloud of dust rose up in the air. The R.I.V., which had been the target, and the church both remained intact, but the villa was severely damaged. The two wings at opposite ends, the one where Aniceta's and Virginia's rooms had once been and the other one where Clara's room was, were partly destroyed. In less than five minutes, a large portion of the personal objects that these three Agnelli women had accumulated in Villar Perosa had been lost in a cloud of smoke and dust.

The death of Virginia Agnelli in an automobile accident in November 1945 was followed a few weeks later by that of the *senatore.* Clara Agnelli died a few months after that. Their deaths shortly after the end of the war spelled a sudden end to an era of fundamental expansion and vitality in the history of Villar Perosa and the Agnelli family.

Russell Page and Villar Perosa

Ownership of Villar Perosa, the "home for a lifetime," was bequeathed to Gianni, the preferred grandchild, who was the eldest of Edoardo's children. In addition, the *senatore* bestowed numerous other properties upon him, favoring him over his siblings and cousins. At the age of twenty-four, he consequently became the undisputed head of the family.

The Agnellis at this time were a family of orphans, the majority of them still minors, who were living their lives in uncertainty and experiencing one of the darkest periods they could remember. Chaos and confusion were everywhere and, from their factories to their houses, there was nothing but ruins. In addition to the thousand and one difficulties of that period, Gianni was faced with having to rebuild the two houses that had been badly damaged during the air raids. First there was the enormous nineteenth-century town house at Corso Oporto, recently renamed Corso Matteotti, which dated to the time of King Umberto I. It was the home where Gianni had been born and where he had grown up. And then there was the Villar Perosa residence, which was now his property. The chief gardener, Gaetano Aloisio, had managed with the help of his assistant gardeners to remove most of the rubble and debris from the lawns and the plants. Gianni had given orders that the rebuilding and restoring should be done as quickly as possible. He would stop by to inspect the progress of the work, which was monitored daily by Agostino Stella, the *senatore's* butler, who had remained at his post. Gaetano had meanwhile resolutely taken the reins of his garden in hand again.

Nonetheless, the estate, located far away among the mountains, was not a suitable place for a young bachelor to live. Up until then he had never lived in the house without his grandparents being there as well. All too vivid remembrances of other times, echoes of voices that had only just been silenced, and memories that were too tangible made the beautiful dwelling a less than carefree place to stay. "During those years, the Avvocato came here infrequently and, when he came, he did not stay long," recalls Guido Pascal, one of Gaetano Aloisio's young assistants. When the latter retired, Pascal took his place and worked for Gianni and Marella for just as many years, as Gaetano had for Aniceta and later for the *senatore.*

Meanwhile the seasons came and went. Agostino Stella, the old maid Mina, and Agnese in the linen room with her assistants all maintained the house impeccably, and Gaetano Aloisio did just about the same in the garden. But he did take liberties in some of the things he did, especially when he emphasized the exotic, which probably not even Aniceta would have liked and which Russell Page later found so distasteful.

The senatore *with his grandson Gianni, circa 1940.*

The Villa Agnelli is called after a famous Italian family, who still inhabit it during occasional holidays and the late summer months.

With all their many other properties and interests, it occupies a very special place in the family's affections, and the care and taste with which Signora Agnelli has restored it after the damage done in the last war have not only saved for Italy a house of exceptional interest, but have created an atmosphere within it and around it which is among the most perfect described in this book.

—Nigel Nicolson, *Great Houses,* 1968

Russell Page arrived at Villar Perosa in 1955, on a beautiful day at the end of June. Despite the summer heat, the terraced fields and the grassy slopes that could be seen from the car windows were a glossy green. The mountain peaks, which soon became visible, still showed some traces of snow; on arrival at his destination, the air was clear and crisp. Next to him, on the leather seat of the chauffeur-driven dark blue Fiat, sat Stéphane Boudin, an old friend of Page, who was a famous and much respected interior decorator and the director of the Maison Jansen. The invitation to consider Villar Perosa more carefully had been made at the suggestion of Boudin. After he had worked for some time in the Agnelli home in Turin, Gianni and Marella had asked him to see what improvements could be made to Villar. Some of the interior spaces damaged by the 1944 bombings had already been restored, and others were still practically intact from the time of Clara Agnelli at the beginning of the second decade of the century. During his many visits, Boudin had made numerous suggestions, most of which had been well received. The most important of these had been to reopen the main veranda at the rear of the house, which had been partly closed at one time in order to build some bathrooms there, and subsequently to rebuild the main bedrooms completely. While they walked around the house discussing the possibilities for improving it, Marella Agnelli recalls many years later, Boudin kept going to the windows to look outside. He finally expressed his feeling that one of the most important aspects of Villar was its views of the garden and that the garden was what they should really concentrate on. The garden, he urged, needed to be restored.

It was at this point that Boudin had mentioned the name of Russell Page. Marella Agnelli, who did not know Page personally at the time, was particularly eager to follow this advice and make several changes in the garden. In fact, she knew and appreciated his work because she had specifically gone to see the Loggia, the garden that Theofilo Rossi di Montelera was having designed by Page near Turin.

Like Aniceta before her, Marella understood that Villar gave something to the family that no other house, no matter how luxurious and beautiful, could ever have provided. It was an old, spacious, and elegant home and, at the same time, a domestic world full of memories and traditions. Located close to Turin, it was also accessible not only during the summer but also during the weekends of the in-between seasons. As Marella recalls,

> *I remember when I first went to Villar right after I was married, I was enchanted by the timeless atmosphere that still prevailed in the house. There were these devoted ladies, Mina and Agnese, who worked there. They wore long aprons and finely embroidered camisoles.*
>
> *Supervising everything was Agostino Stella, once the senatore's butler, who saw to it that everything remained as it had been at the time of Clara and the senatore. The house had remained closed after the air raids of 1944, and the part that had not been damaged by the bombs had remained magically intact.*
>
> *Even more beautiful than the house was the garden, because it had retained the atmosphere of times past. The intentional eccentric combination of formality and domesticity and the variety of overlapping styles made it stand out and gave it an extremely pleasant and original look.*

In *Education of a Gardener,* however, Russell Page relates how surprised he was to find himself in a garden that was too small in proportion to the house and too suffocated and burdened with nineteenth-century memories. "Wherever there was level ground," he wrote with disapproval, "there was a formal parterre—there were a total of six—some terraced and all emphasized by endless rows of ugly terracotta vases, fountains and white marble statues." For years the gardener had continued to plant conifers and add flower beds, for the most part with sage and red geraniums. The garden had become overgrown and lacking harmony. Gaetano Aloisio had been working at Villar for more than half a century. Once it had been abandoned to his skilled and loving hands, it had become the garden of the gardener. It would seem that nothing could have been more contrary to Page's sophisticated austerity and his love of broad and clear-cut spaces.

Villar Perosa immediately appealed to Page's imagination. At first, Marella recalls, he got excited by the idea of creating a mountain garden. Later, once he understood the potential value of this place with its broad surfaces and its privileged location, he was stimulated by the difficult task and the unusual challenge it posed. In fact, Villar did not need to be restored to what it had once been; at the same time, it was not possible to make a clean slate and start from scratch.

In this particular place prevailed the powerful, and by now well-established, structure of Aniceta's garden. There were too many invisible ties that bound this family of owners to the past, their past, which was still present here and there in the garden. Marella felt the presence of these ties as well, and she did her best to preserve their spirit and their most peculiar and original aspects.

The challenge Page faced was therefore twofold. He had to give a new identity to the garden while, at the same time, preserving its tradition and structure.

During his first visit to Villar Perosa, Page slowly walked around the garden in a quiet and reflective mood. He inspected all of it, starting with the lawn in front of the house. On that first day, Page also spent considerable time visiting the house and appraising the views of the landscape from the windows and from the open verandas and balconies. He did this to try to get an idea of the entire panorama and the various perspectives. From time to time, he would jot down a few notes or trace a rough sketch on a small notepad he kept in his pocket.

Page said at once that the vegetation was too dense and that the trees obstructed the splendid view of the landscape. The uneven quality of the garden did not do justice to the light and graceful architecture of the house. The most urgent step to be taken was to recapture the feeling of spaciousness. The objective was to unburden the garden and open it up to the landscape, the mountains, and the sky.

That evening, before dinner, drinks were served in the portico. While Stéphane Boudin chatted with the Avvocato, Marella and Russell Page were standing close to the iron railing and looking at the garden that stretched out in front of them. It was a mild evening and they could hear the gurgling of water and the croaking of the frogs. Marella recalls, "At that moment, just before sunset, Page said something that surprised me and which touched me profoundly. . . . While talking candidly about the dangers to which an individual is exposed who suddenly finds himself or herself surrounded by great riches, he said, 'We must not forget that we are here to serve something greater than us all, for otherwise we risk becoming slaves to whatever is most base and material in our lives.'"

That unexpected observation, made by an old master of the art of gardening to a young apprentice, marked the beginning of a long, fruitful, and intense collaboration, which was nonetheless often full of contention and conflict. For Marella Agnelli, the creation of the garden was the beginning of a long journey.

The garden of Villar would become something more valuable and more complex than simply a beautiful and natural extension of the house.

"From the garden, any garden, one receives not only a sense of beauty; one receives also a sense of peace, of open vision, of spirituality. In the course of these years," remarks Marella, "I have often retreated to a garden during difficult moments. The contact with nature, with living plants, has been and continues to be a great comfort."

One of the first changes was the removal of the old fence so as to extend the boundaries in order to include some fields where apples and cherries had always been grown. From the villa's upper windows their thick pink and white blossoms can be seen every spring.

But after the first concrete and visible steps had been taken, the journey that led to the remaking of Villar became fraught with difficulties. Between one success and the next, the garden turned into a battlefield of differing and often conflicting intentions.

Gaetano Aloisio had enjoyed almost unlimited freedom. And, as was the custom in many Italian gardens of the time, the head gardener made most of the decisions regarding the garden. For example, the gardener chose not only the juxtapositions and the intensities of the colors, but also the shape of the flower beds and the borders. Each year he dictated where and how the numerous potted plants were to be placed.

Gaetano was a diligent worker who was devoted to the Agnelli family and to Villar Perosa. On the occasion of his fortieth anniversary of service, the *senatore* had expressed his gratitude and that of the family by presenting him with a beautiful gold medal. Yet just a decade later, Gaetano perceived Page's arrival as a catastrophe that would destroy the perfect little world he had created over the previous fifty years.

"Every fir tree, every monkey-puzzle," Page would write in *Education of a Gardener,* "had been planted by this man who grew gloomier and gloomier as they were cut down one by one. In the end I was able to eliminate the majority of the formal gardens, put all the statues and pots out of my sight, get rid of the winding gravel paths that led nowhere and, finally, see daylight."

But the road to "daylight," as Page soon found out, was not a smooth one. The story goes that after Page's routing of the garden, Gaetano would return everything the way it had been—and that he was firmly supported in this by Marella Agnelli herself. The plants would not be cut and the pots would be returned to their places as soon as Page's car rounded the first turn on the way back to Turin.

The foremost problem was one of communication. Page did not speak Italian and had difficulty making himself understood by the gardeners. And they, on the other hand, did not make the slightest effort. At times, when no one was around to translate for him, Page would in desperation resort to gestures. The gardeners, relates Guido Pascal, could not help laughing at the sight of this giant of a man running back and forth

Russell Page at Villar Perosa, 1958.

and gesticulating like a madman in an attempt to make himself understood. "Our laughter was something he could not bear," Pascal remembers with a smile. "He would explode with rage, his eyes darting like flames. . . . I don't think he ever forgave us."

From then on, feeling secure in the support of his assistants and Marella, Gaetano Aloisio began challenging almost every order he was given. There was the famous question of the roots, for example. Gaetano would cut away part of a plant's roots when transplanting it. But according to Page, this was sometimes done too drastically and in such a way as to endanger the plant itself. It would infuriate Page, but to no avail. "I even cut the roots of onions," Gaetano would often say, "and here comes this Englishman and tells me I must not do so."

As time went by and Page established more and more control, however, Gaetano became increasingly irritable and intractable. Villar and its ancient structure, its traditions and its spirit, were battling the changes proposed by Page. Marella had to make a clear decision, and she did: No radical transformation could be imposed on an entity so overflowing with vitality and personality. And, after working faithfully for so many years, Gaetano could not, and should not, be deprived of authority or sacrificed for the holy cause of "renewal."

Marella, who was so much younger than Page and had little experience in gardening, started out as a pupil who was devoted to the old maestro and eager to learn from him. But as the project called for other old

Gianni and Marella Agnelli, Villar Perosa, 1986.

trees to be cut down and for part of the old gardens to be uprooted, she began to resist. "As soon as I put my foot down, so to speak, the fights started," remembers Marella.

They had many disagreements and differences of opinion, but there was one notable clash in particular. It was about a small wood of fir trees that closed off the garden at the back of the villa. It had been planted at the end of the nineteenth century by Aniceta, and over the years the trees had grown into a massive green wall that completely blotted out the view of the mountains and the valley. Without consulting Marella, and taking advantage of the fact that she and Gianni were away on a trip, Page ordered the trees cut down; by the time she found out, they were gone. She managed to save only the three or four that had not yet been cut. "I felt very sad about it," Marella recalls. "I could not reconcile myself with the fact that he had cut down trees and things that had been there for years and years, generations even, and which, at least to my eyes, were full of meaning. Page, on the other hand, made a strictly aesthetic evaluation devoid of sentimentalism."

This last energetic and unexpected cleaning up of the garden brought the conflict between Marella and Russell to a head. There was a long and animated discussion, which took place on Aniceta's wooden bridge in the garden at Villar. The breakup was resolved by Page's promise not to touch Aniceta's garden in any way, but instead to concentrate on a completely new project, with a proposal for the valley below that same bridge —

outside of and far from the boundaries of the old garden. The Lake Valley was born as a promise of peace and an ultimate token of confidence in a profound, though troubled and saddened, friendship.

The valley was small, narrow, and deep, almost a gorge, and it was practically inaccessible. There was a small stream at the bottom, and a dense vegetation of acacias and blackberry bushes grew along the sides.

It was not long before Page's proposal was accepted and the biggest job could begin, the one that can be described as the masterpiece of the collaboration between Russell and Marella.

This area, known as *i laghi* (the Lakes) for its succession of eleven artificial lakes, represents the perfect balance between Page's grandiose conception and Marella's sensibility.

Since the valley is located on sloping terrain, it was decided to build a series of small dams that would channel the stream water toward the succession of small lakes, which would all be different in size and shape. Page spent many hours overseeing the work and taking photographs, some of which have been preserved in the archives of the Royal Horticultural Society in London. As a gardener used to working with his hands, he was fascinated by the craftsmanship of the local workers—mountain people who instinctively knew how to build walls and dams with rocks, branches, and mud. "I was amazed at the rapidity and skill with which they would translate a rough sketch into a solid construction," he would write many years later in *Education of a Gardener*. "Walls, waterfalls, steps and paving seemed to go up almost as fast as I could draw them."

The Lake Valley at Villar Perosa constitutes a perfect balance between the water and the rocks and the rich, imaginative, and often exotic combination of the plants and flowers with the surrounding landscape. Access to the lakes is via the wooden bridge, which Page redesigned to replace the one built there by Aniceta. The bridge crosses a steep ravine, which is moist and dark and filled with rhododendrons, azaleas, and Japanese maples. In the shadiest part grow *Vinca minor,* jonquils, and tassel hyacinths, which in spring cover the ground with carpets of bright and vibrant colors.

From the bridge, a path leads to the top of the valley, where the succession of water pools begins. The view from here is wide open and striking—one sees a large valley divided by small lakes covered with water lilies, grasses, and aquatic plants. To one side is an expanse of manicured lawns bordered by a series of shrubs planted in groups. Above the broad, winding borders of herbaceous plants stand clumps of bamboo, star magnolias, hydrangeas, specimen roses, and, finally, broad and abundant Japanese cornels.

The result is a wide, airy landscape, full of movement, unrestrained in color and structure, which helps to create an unusual contrast with the rest of the garden.

"When we first set out to design the Valley of the Lakes," Marella recalls, "Russell was very excited at the prospect of creating a garden of native plants, an Alpine garden. But as time went by, we were soon doing the opposite and planting herbaceous plants, shrubs, and trees from all over the world, from China, from Japan, from North and South America."

To close off the valley on one side, Page proposed a spacious garden with variegated leaves that would be located under the terraces to the south and under the avenue of the Japanese cherry trees. The focal point of the garden is an old common catalpa, with its scented summer blossoms. The sides are closed off by an ancient boxwood hedge. In the early 1990s, this garden was widened, renewed, and restored by Marella Agnelli with the help of Paolo Pejrone, a pupil of Page. Grasses and bamboos, as well as shrubs, all with variegated leaves, were brought in to take the place of an extremely large parterre of *Hosta aureomarginata.*

Until the mid-1980s, the garden of Villar Perosa remained as it had been modified by Marella and Page. Around that time, the architect Gae Aulenti was given the task of submitting a proposal for a swimming pool and ancillary structures in a sheltered corner at the back of the park. These new additions, located on a slope at a point that commands a view of the Val Chisone and the surrounding mountains, give a lively and contemporary touch to the garden.

A rocky path crosses a miniature hill covered with ferns and countless species of heather that end in front of a wooden pavilion. The wooden columns support the weight of a solid but elegant structure of deceptive simplicity.

Aulenti describes the project in this way:

The intent had been to create a "natural" architecture that, by juxtaposing various raw materials, stone and wood in particular, would be in harmony with the surrounding landscape and the gardens, and which would constitute an ideally essential and suitable environment as well for the placement of a collection of large bronze sculptures of contemporary artists.

While working with Marella on several projects, I was especially impressed by the perception she was able to form of the finished garden. She is able to imagine it as it will be years from now. I believe that she can do this because she has a very trained eye. She loves art and she has been a dedicated photographer for years. Contrary to many experts in the area of gardening, who give priority to considerations from the botanical point of view, Marella has always had a feeling for form, color, and composition.

Over the past decade, Marella Agnelli has devoted much time, together with Paolo Pejrone, to creating a garden that would complement the work of Gae Aulenti. Heathers and ferns, ceanothi and pampas grasses, spireas and guelder roses, all soften the harsh lines of the wooden houses.

The rounded forms of enormous pruned boxwoods, some in pots, others in long rows along one side of the pool, give the setting a keen formality. On one side, close to the wooden pavilion, is a raised "miniature" garden, which is closed off by a wall covered by densely planted iceberg roses.

A large bronze fountain sculpture by Magritte stands out against the background. It represents a female torso, from which flows a constant veil of water. A spacious lawn stretches along the side of the hill and slopes down to the valley. All the way at the end and marking the garden's boundary, there looms a gigantic sculpture by Henry Moore identified as *Bone*. The presence of these and other statues is a tribute to the collection that Gianni Agnelli has put together over a period of more than forty years.

The corner with the swimming pool was created to satisfy the wishes of a growing number of grand-children, the eight children of Margherita Agnelli de Pahlen, daughter of Gianni and Marella Agnelli. Like previous generations of the family, Margherita's children spend a few weeks with their grandparents at Villar Perosa every year, usually in September. But the most regular visitor of all is Edoardo Agnelli, who visits year-round.

The garden of Villar Perosa is now in the expert hands of Oscar Deval, the chief gardener, who has taken the place of Guido Pascal, Gaetano Aloisio's successor. Every year it is necessary to perform some small restoration. Most recently, for example, the vegetable garden was cleaned up and put in order. In 1997 the Avenue of the Horse Chestnuts was reorganized and replanted. Three years earlier, a cleaning and revision of the lakes was needed.

It is in fact the combination of change and continuity that makes the gardens fascinating and unusual. When one looks back over the history of Villar Perosa, the thread of continuity seems very visible indeed and can still be found in many corners and in the many individual gardens there.

As Marella remembers, "Several years later, when the garden was finally completed, I visited the garden together with Russell, who came for one of his usual inspection visits. As we were walking, I suddenly remembered our original plan and I asked him, 'Russell, whatever happened to your idea of creating a sponta-neous garden of native plants?' 'Oh,' he replied with an enigmatic smile, 'but Villar is different from all other gardens. . . . It is my Shangri-la, my ideal world.'"

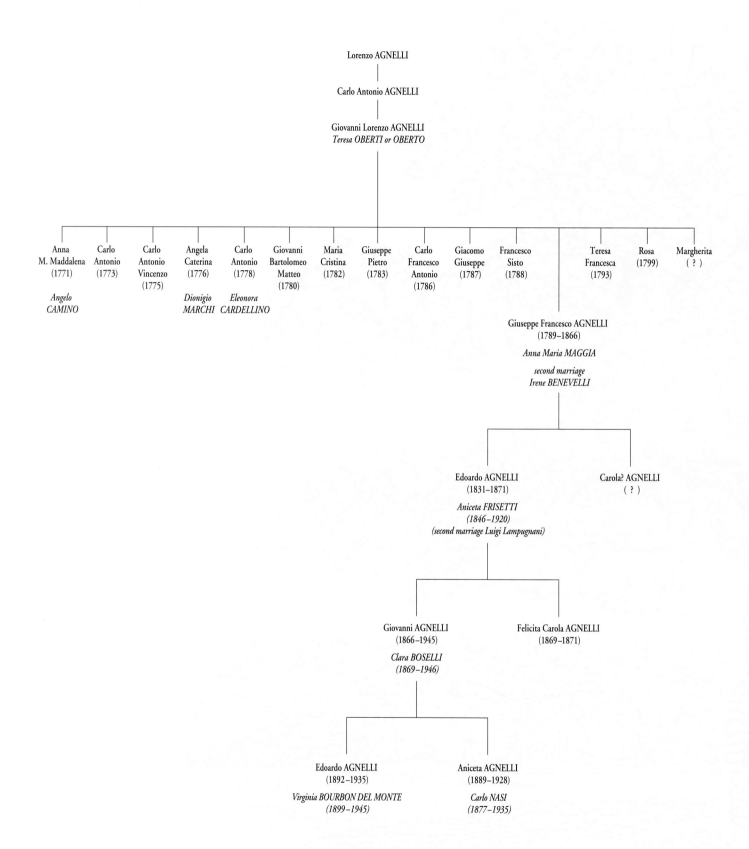

Lorenzo AGNELLI

Carlo Antonio AGNELLI

Giovanni Lorenzo AGNELLI
Teresa OBERTI or OBERTO

Anna
M. Maddalena
(1771)

*Angelo
CAMINO*

Carlo
Antonio
(1773)

Carlo
Antonio
Vincenzo
(1775)

Angela
Caterina
(1776)

*Dionigio
MARCHI*

Carlo
Antonio
(1778)

*Eleonora
CARDELLINO*

Giovanni
Bartolomeo
Matteo
(1780)

Maria
Cristina
(1782)

Giuseppe
Pietro
(1783)

Carlo
Francesco
Antonio
(1786)

Giacomo
Giuseppe
(1787)

Francesco
Sisto
(1788)

Teresa
Francesca
(1793)

Rosa
(1799)

Margherita
(?)

Giuseppe Francesco AGNELLI
(1789–1866)

Anna Maria MAGGIA

*second marriage
Irene BENEVELLI*

Edoardo AGNELLI
(1831–1871)

*Aniceta FRISETTI
(1846–1920)
(second marriage Luigi Lampugnani)*

Carola? AGNELLI
(?)

Giovanni AGNELLI
(1866–1945)

*Clara BOSELLI
(1869–1946)*

Felicita Carola AGNELLI
(1869–1871)

Edoardo AGNELLI
(1892–1935)

*Virginia BOURBON DEL MONTE
(1899–1945)*

Aniceta AGNELLI
(1889–1928)

*Carlo NASI
(1877–1935)*

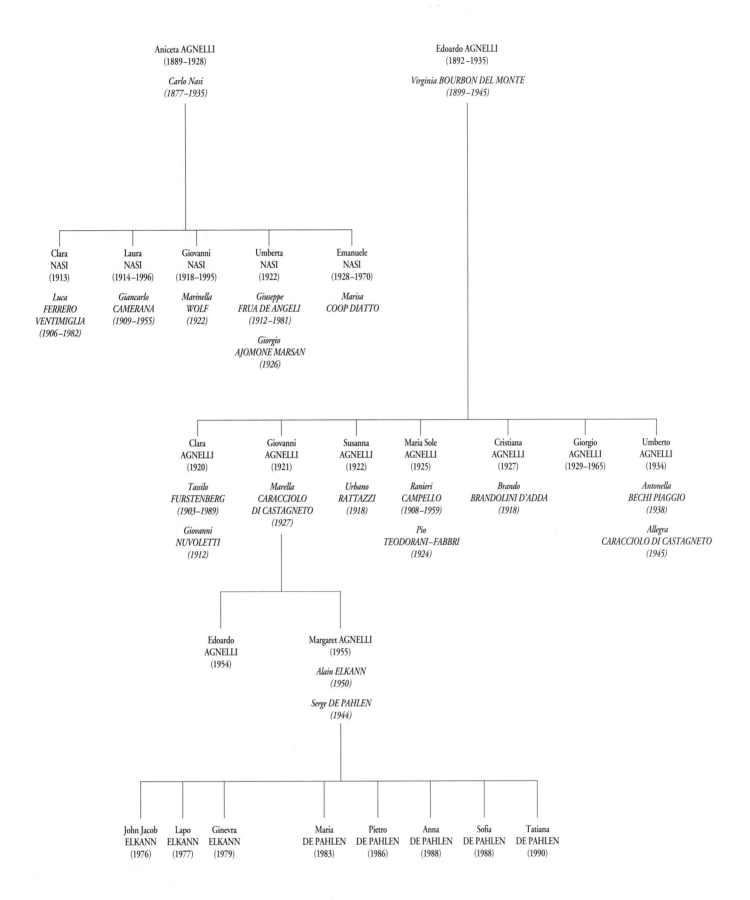

Aniceta AGNELLI
(1889–1928)

Carlo Nasi
(1877–1935)

Edoardo AGNELLI
(1892–1935)

Virginia BOURBON DEL MONTE
(1899–1945)

Clara
NASI
(1913)

Luca
FERRERO
VENTIMIGLIA
(1906–1982)

Laura
NASI
(1914–1996)

Giancarlo
CAMERANA
(1909–1955)

Giovanni
NASI
(1918–1995)

Marinella
WOLF
(1922)

Umberta
NASI
(1922)

Giuseppe
FRUA DE ANGELI
(1912–1981)

Giorgio
AJOMONE MARSAN
(1926)

Emanuele
NASI
(1928–1970)

Marisa
COOP DIATTO

Clara
AGNELLI
(1920)

Tassilo
FURSTENBERG
(1903–1989)

Giovanni
NUVOLETTI
(1912)

Giovanni
AGNELLI
(1921)

Marella
CARACCIOLO
DI CASTAGNETO
(1927)

Susanna
AGNELLI
(1922)

Urbano
RATTAZZI
(1918)

Maria Sole
AGNELLI
(1925)

Ranieri
CAMPELLO
(1908–1959)

Pio
TEODORANI–FABBRI
(1924)

Cristiana
AGNELLI
(1927)

Brando
BRANDOLINI D'ADDA
(1918)

Giorgio
AGNELLI
(1929–1965)

Umberto
AGNELLI
(1934)

Antonella
BECHI PIAGGIO
(1938)

Allegra
CARACCIOLO DI CASTAGNETO
(1945)

Edoardo
AGNELLI
(1954)

Margaret AGNELLI
(1955)

Alain ELKANN
(1950)

Serge DE PAHLEN
(1944)

John Jacob
ELKANN
(1976)

Lapo
ELKANN
(1977)

Ginevra
ELKANN
(1979)

Maria
DE PAHLEN
(1983)

Pietro
DE PAHLEN
(1986)

Anna
DE PAHLEN
(1988)

Sofia
DE PAHLEN
(1988)

Tatiana
DE PAHLEN
(1990)

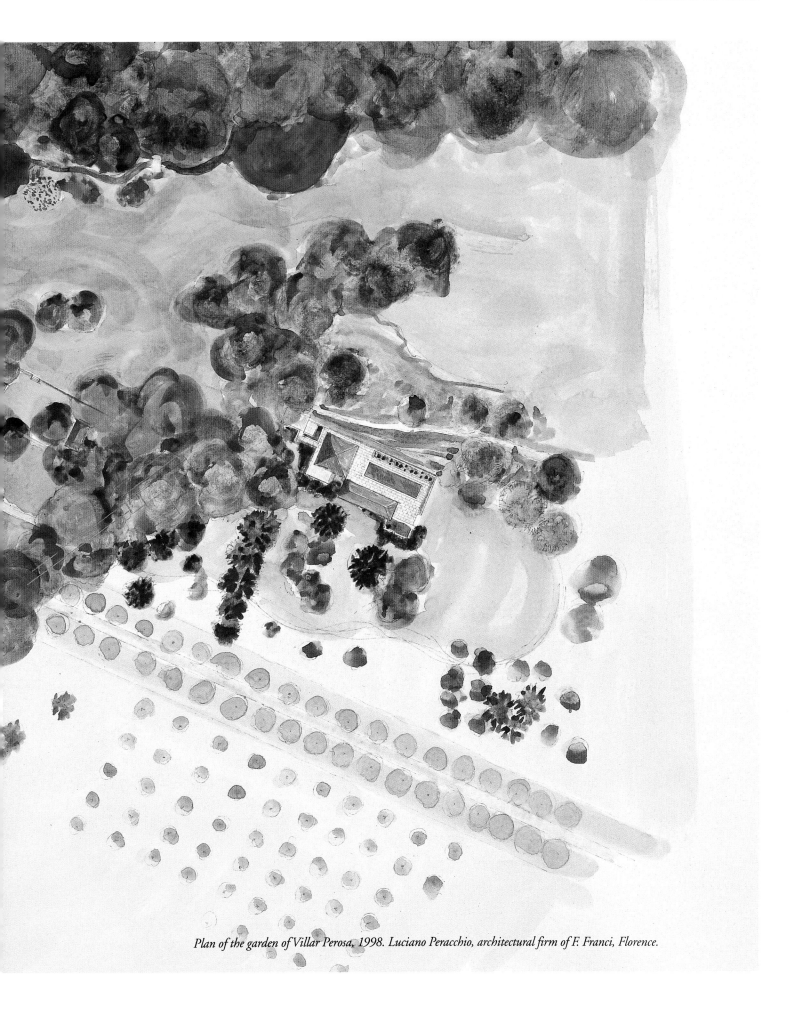

Plan of the garden of Villar Perosa, 1998. Luciano Peracchio, architectural firm of F. Franci, Florence.

The Avenue of the Horse Chestnuts

A long avenue of old horse chestnuts, *Aesculus hippocastanum,* along which young tulip trees have been planted, *Liriodendron tulipifera,* connects the garden of the villa—which has always been known as the "Castle"—with its ancient gate.

Fields of mature apple trees, *Malus communis,* flank the chestnuts. The Arcadian serenity of the landscape is punctuated by dense groupings of cedars of Lebanon, *Cedrus libani.* Knowing that the apple trees would die out over time, Russell Page arranged to have numerous cedars of Lebanon planted with the intent of providing a strong contrast to the harsh mountain landscape.

Over the past few years, the horse chestnuts have also shown signs of poor aging and in the future they will be replaced by tulip trees. This change of plantings is prudent since it's best to avoid planting trees of the same family, genus, and species in the same places.

The "Castle" is hidden by the old trees in the park. An allée of horse chestnuts, Aesculus hippocastanum, *joins the nearby villa garden to the gate.*

The Main Facade

The main facade, attributed to the architect Filippo Juvarra, overlooks the Chisone Valley. The wide plateau is bordered by the narrow, shady gorges of Porto and Fenestrelle.

The house is flanked by two verandas, each enclosed by large windows. Scissor-shaped stairs, typical of Juvarra's style, were added during the early eighteenth century.

A spacious garden typical of the nineteenth century opens up in front of the main facade. Araucarias, *Araucaria araucana,* sequoias, *Sequoia sempervirens,* magnolias, *Magnolia grandiflora,* and linden trees, *Tilia europaea,* were planted there at the end of the nineteenth century, thanks to the gardening passion of Mrs. Agnelli Lampugnani, mother of the founder of Fiat.

Eight Piedmontese-type planting boxes with laurels, *Laurus nobilis,* pruned to resemble small trees, and a large olea fragrans, *Osmanthus fragrans,* which stands close to the south corner, decorate the facade; old cross vines, *Bignonia capreolata,* thickly cover the pilasters.

An araucaria, Araucaria araucana, *thuja,* Thuja occidentalis, *and other small trees located on the western front of the villa.*

An iced-over pond positioned directly in the center of the garden before the main entrance.

Opposite: The araucaria, Araucaria araucana, *a plant originally from the Andes,
thrives at Villar Perosa.*

Preceding spread: An old linden tree, Tilia europaea, *and small pond with a single jet of water.
Planters with exquisitely pruned laurels,* Laurus nobilis, *add a note of formality.*

Harsh winter light emphasizes the severe lines of the Juvarra-style architecture.

The East Front

Two floors of open verandas front the eastern facade and overlook the garden, including some beech trees and the Lake Valley. The pilasters of the verandas are covered by very old cross vines, *Bignonia capreolata.* Four beds bordered by boxwood, *Buxus sempervirens,* form the boundaries of the parterre together with two high pyramid-shaped yews, *Taxus baccata.* A meadow sloping down toward the Lake Valley flanks a small wood of age-old beeches, *Fagus sylvatica.* On the north, the villa is bordered by the terrace with the lemon conservatory and by the Magnolia Terrace. The green dome of the church of S. Pietro in Vincoli completes the view.

The eastern side of the house opens onto a large meadow; it is closed off by the Italian Gardens to the south and rose gardens to the north.

The snow-covered garden looking west.

Preceding spread: An azalea 'Palestrina', Rhododendron 'Palestrina', *ornamental apple trees and magnolias,*
Magnolia semperflorens, *are offset by a stand of beeches in the background.*

In the summer creeping cross vines, Bignonia capreolata, *cover the pilasters on both floors of the verandas.*

The east facade and, in the foreground, azaleas in bloom.

A jonquil meadow in bloom.

Overleaf: In the shade of a stunning magnolia, Magnolia semperflorens, *a staircase, set off by two marble vases, joins the immediate garden with the Magnolia Terrace and the Lemon Conservatory. The majestic silhouette of the church of S. Pietro in Vincoli looms in the background.*

The Chapel and the Tower

The little chapel with its pleasing Neo-Gothic design, dedicated to the marchioness Incontri, is framed by two big yew trees, *Taxus baccata,* and an ancient hedge of boxwood, *Buxus sempervirens.* A nineteenth-century water tower, blanketed by ivy, *Hedera helix,* and bordered by large cedars of Lebanon, *Cedrus libani,* and thujas, *Thuja gegantea,* provides a romantic view and terminus to this older part of the garden. The trees were planted in the mid-1800s in accordance with the eclectic and exotic taste of the times.

The family chapel is nestled in a surround of araucarias, Araucaria araucana, *yews,* Taxus baccata, *cedars of Lebanon,* Cedrus libani, *and thujas,* Thuja occidentalis, *and linden trees,* Tilia europaea.

The Bridge

The wooden bridge, first planned by Aniceta Agnelli, was subsequently redesigned by Russell Page, who had been inspired by the Chinese-style structures of British architect Sir William Chambers. The bridge serves to connect the banks of the little valley; this practical necessity also has resulted in an extremely scenic and attractive vista.

The entire area is shaded by enormous beeches, *Fagus sylvatica.* Ferns, small bulbous rhododendrons, *Rhododendron loderi,* camellias, *Camellia japonica, Ruscus racemosus,* and some forsythia add color to the shady undergrowth in the early spring.

From the bridge, one has a commanding view of the Lake Valley. Hydrangea bushes, *Hydrangea sargentiana,* and white azaleas 'Palestrina', *Rhododendron 'Palestrina',* cover the riverbed and spread out around the edges of the bridge.

Fagus sylvatica, *and oak trees,* Quercus, *are part of the woodland garden winding in and around Page's elegant bridge.*

Rhododendrons, Rhododendron loderi, *and camellias,* Camellia japonica, *clusters of small maples,* Acer,
and ferns fill in the meandering garden.

Facing page: From the bridge one has a spectacular and unobstructed view of the Lake Valley.

The bridge and surrounding foliage as seen during various times of the year.

Towering beech trees, Fagus sylvatica.

Preceding spread: A coating of snow transforms the Chinese-style bridge and plantings into a scene of quiet beauty.

Rhododendrons, azaleas, Japanese maples, ferns, and, in the background, the Chinese-style bridge.

Overleaf: The brilliant red of the azalea amoena, Rhododendron kiusianum *var.* japonicum, *are a dramatic counterpoint to the beeches,* Fagus sylvatica.

The Lake Valley

This valley, designed and created by Russell Page in the early 1950s, is especially striking from August to October. Before Page intervened, a steep and impenetrable irrigation ditch allowed one to guess at, rather than to see, the presence of a small mountain stream as it flowed down the length of the Chisone Valley. Today, about twenty small lakes meander down a slight incline. The roar of numerous short waterfalls and the refreshing view of the clear water are the constant companions of the visitor.

In addition to large groups of bamboo, magnolias, hydrangeas, *Ruscus,* flowering cherries, and rosebushes are numerous botanically significant plants.

Water lilies, Nymphaea, *and pontederie,* Pontederia cordata,
as well as carp, abound in the lakes.
The banks are often covered with massive ferns. In the background are
Caryopteris clandonensis *with their soothing lavender flowers. Water flows*
past the shade of a large guelder rose, Viburnum rhytidophyllum.

Old plane trees define the borders of Aniceta's garden and the new Lake Valley.

Preceding spread: Guelder roses, Viburnum plicatum *'Mariesii', cast reflections in the water.*
Japanese azalea shrubs, Rhododendron japonica, *offset the roses with fragrant yellow flowers.*

An autumnal view of the Cornus kousa chinensis *trees.*

The pink cornus, Cornus florida rubra, *in bloom.*

Preceding pages 136–39: The Japanese dogwood trees, Cornus kousa, *which in June are
covered with white bracts are replaced by red, strawberry-shaped fruit in September.*

In March, the star magnolias, Magnolia stellata, *are the first early spring flowers to bloom.*
A large Japanese pagoda tree, Sophora japonica, *looms behind.*

Just when the Sargent cherry trees, with their delicate pink flowers, Prunus sargentii, *bloom at the end of March, the Katsura trees,* Cercidiphyllum japonicum, *come into leaf.*

Pages 144–49: The ferns, sky-blue irises, Iris sibirica, *bamboo,* Phyllostachys, *and the gunnera,* Gunnera manicata, *all thrive on the moist terrain around the lake banks.*

A waterfall laps the guelder roses, Viburnum plicatum *'Mariesii', and the*
Mahonias, Mahonia japonica; *on the left is a field of irises,* Iris sibirica.

Opposite: The tall trees of the valley, planted by Russell Page, are reflected among
the water lilies, Nymphaea, *and the pontederie,* Pontederia cordata.

Overleaf: The zebra-striped leaves of the miscanthus, Miscanthus sinensis 'Zebrinus',
are light and almost transparent in the strong rays of the August sun.

An autumn view of one of the many lakes.

Opposite: The dogwood forests, Cornus stolonifera, *of Villar Perosa
turn red in the fall. Huge dawn redwoods,* Metasequoia glyptostroboides,
are reflected in the water.

Preceding spread: A stunning gunnera, Gunnera manicata.

Astilbe, Astilbe arendsii, *and, opposite, a group of ferns,* Matteuccia struthiopteris.

Preceding spread: A sweeping view of the magnificent Lake Valley.

The Avenue of the Hornbeams

In accordance with Marella Agnelli's wishes, an avenue of densely planted hornbeams, *Carpinus betulus fastigiata,* which have been pruned to resemble pyramids, skirts one of the entranceways to the garden. Hidden from the visitor who uses the avenue is a large area dedicated to flowers for cutting on one side and, on the other, the vegetable garden. This garden has always been impeccably cared for and it has always been one of the most enchanting parts of the gardens.

Over time, the Avenue of the Hornbeams has become the easiest access road to the "Castle." A forbidding gate, flanked by two solid pilasters capped with pointed Neo-Gothic spires, separates the garden from the avenue.

Opposite and overleaf: The carefully pruned hornbeams,
Carpinus fastigiata, *border the avenue that leads to Villar Perosa.*

Views of the Church

The dazzlingly bright facade of the Juvarra-style church of S. Pietro in Vincoli faces west and looks out over the Avenue of the Hornbeams and the vegetable garden. A steep cobblestone road connects it with the underlying plain of the "Castle."

In front of the church portals is a large, fan-shaped panoramic square that is solidly built like a terrace. The house of the vicar, which is a small and solid building, is located along the south end of the square. The joyful sound of church bells marks the hours of the day and is heard in every part of the "Castle" garden.

The church of S. Pietro in Vincoli was probably designed by Filippo Juvarra. The stately Avenue of the Hornbeams, Carpinus fastigiata, *is prominently featured in the foreground.*

Overleaf: The church seen from the Magnolia Terrace. A stately cedar tree from the Himalayas, Cedrus deodara, *closes off the terrace on the left.*

On the preceding spread and these pages: The Juvarra-style church of S. Pietro in Vincoli seen throughout the year.

The Lemon Conservatory

On a large terrace stands a nineteenth-century lemon conservatory. Citrus trees, long an important feature in Italian and Piedmontese gardens, are the perfect solace for a winter refuge.

In the middle of a large rose garden is a circular pond surrounded by thriving bergenia, *Bergenia crassifolia*. It is in this rose garden that the many roses to be cut for decorating the "Castle" are grown. Particular attention is given to the cultivation of two kinds of roses, the 'Donna Marella Agnelli' and the 'Marella Agnelli', two cultivars of pink roses, one from the firm of Barni in Pistoria and the other from Meilland in Le Luc in Provence.

The oldest and weakest rosebushes are replaced every year with hardier bushes. The soil is likewise replaced so that the new plants grow in rich and virus-free terrain when still young. Each year the rose garden is treated with large but balanced quantities of fertilizer. It is also thanks to this careful nurturing that the roses of Villar Perosa are especially fragrant and typically resistant to disease.

*Here, and on the next spread, the terrace with the Lemon Conservatory is covered
by a cutting garden for roses and topiary boxwood,* Buxus sempervirens.

The Lemon Conservatory was erected in the nineteenth century as a way to keep a year-round supply of citrus plants.

The rose cutting garden off the terrace is highly perfumed.

Overleaf: The fountain bordered by a perfectly shaped rim of bergenia, Bergenia crassifolia.
A large magnolia, Magnolia grandiflora, *partially hides a view of the "Castle."*

The Magnolia Terrace

Two large old magnolias, *Magnolia soulangeana* and *Magnolia stellata,* define the terrace that takes its name from them.

Marella Agnelli and Russell Page surrounded the terrace with a large parterre of 'Zambra' roses enclosed by a perfectly sculpted double row of boxwood, *Buxus sempervirens.* Originally, hibiscus, *Hibiscus syriacus* 'Blue Bird', enclosed the parterre. Over time, however, the plants withered as they grew older and their azure summer blooms became ever less abundant. A few years ago, they were replaced with mounds of boxwood.

Magnolia soulangeana *and* Magnolia stellata *frame the church of S. Pietro in Vincoli.*

Closeup details of Magnolia stellata *and* Magnolia soulangeana *flowers.*

Two Magnolia soulangeana *plants, with different colors, during the month of April.*

Pages 184–85: A sweeping view of the Magnolia Terrace and parterre.

Pages 186–87: Flowering Magnolia soulangeana *with a view of the church of S. Pietro in Vincoli in the background.*

The Italian Gardens

Another part of the garden, just as old, opens up to the south with a series of terraces that appear out of proportion in comparison to the house. They were originally conceived as terraces for vegetable gardens and vineyards but are now an integral and central part of the gardens.

The lower terrace was designed according to a strict Italian layout and planted with boxwood, *Buxus sempervirens,* and roses. Like other areas of the garden, after many years the rose garden was renovated. Creeping roses have been trained up an espalier along the south wall.

In the summer, white begonias, *Begonia semperflorens,* are planted.

The terraces are connected by a wide staircase, which was built with the stone from the Chisone Valley with its characteristic exuberant color. The staircase is flanked by large nineteenth-century vases and ends in a terrace that overlooks the herb garden and the Lake Valley. A marble statue of Diana the Huntress stands above the parterre.

In high summer, the boxwood parterre is planted with roses. Here it
has been planted with white begonias, Begonia semperflorens.

Pages 190–95: Views of the Italian Gardens and the Cherry Tree Allée.

The Cherry Tree Allée

A stunning allée of Japanese cherry trees, *Prunus serrulata* 'Fugenzo', brightens the area during the early days of April and serves as a link between two important parts of the garden. The allée joins the children's playground to the beech tree woodland garden, which is a particularly cool and shady area in summer. Underplantings of periwinkles, *Vinca minor,* are set off by large groups of hydrangeas, *Hydrangea macrophilla* 'Annabelle', and wild tobacco, *Nicotiana sylvestris.* The walls are covered by 'Mermaid' roses, whose deep yellow petals contrast with the cherry trees.

Looking out over the herb garden is a newly made terrace; it's a perfect place to rest and admire the panorama.

A statue of Diana the Huntress amid Japanese cherry trees, Prunus serrulata *'Fugenzo', in bloom.*

Pages 198–201: Near and far views of the Japanese cherry trees, Prunus serrulata *'Fugenzo', as well as the elegant Italian Gardens.*

The Foliage Garden

Russell Page created this display garden, which connects the Cherry Tree Allée with the Lake Valley.

An array of trees and shrubs with variegated leaves includes *Acer negundo* 'variegatum', *Ilex aquifolium* 'Aureo Marginata', *Ligustrum ovalifolium* 'Aureo Marginata', *Elaeagnus pungens* 'Maculata', clumps of variegated dwarf bamboo, *Pleioblastus viridistriatus* var. 'Auricoma' and *Pleioblastus fortunei*, large groups of miscanthus, *Miscanthus sinensis* 'Zebrinus', and other herbaceous plants.

Among the more notable groundcover are *Hosta crispula, Aegopodium podagraria* 'Variegatum', *Phalaris arundinacea* 'Tricolor', *Molinia caerulea* 'Variegata', *Persicaria virginiana* 'Painter's palette', *Hakonechloa macra* 'Aureola', *Pennisetum* orientale, and *Ophiopogon japonicus* 'Variegatus'.

Varying shades of green and textures make up the lower part of the garden.

The Swimming Pool

During the mid-1980s, the architect Gae Aulenti built a swimming pool in the part of the garden that was the least cultivated. The wooden buildings are similar stylistically to houses built in the Chisone Valley. This part of the garden includes commissioned works by modern and contemporary sculptors who were given free rein to express themselves.

The walls and floor of the pool are lined with terracotta tiles that were specially manufactured in Tuscany. Large tiles made of local stone were used to do the flooring of the entire complex. They are bordered by a wide row of boxwood, *Buxus sempervirens,* cut into large mounds and a bed of lavender-colored ageratum, *Ageratum houstonianum.* Spiral plumes of boxwood have been set in terracotta vases.

Special care was given to this part of the garden by Marella Agnelli and by landscape architect Paolo Pejrone.

A bed of ageratum, Ageratum houstonianum, *and boxwood*
plants that have been trimmed to resemble spirals surround the pool.
High up stands a statue by Magritte between the sage plants Salvia farinacea *'Victoria'.*

Lavender-colored ageratum, Ageratum houstonianum, *are massed at one end of the pool.*

Opposite: A sculpture by Caesar among the linden trees.

Overleaf: The elegant family pool and bathhouse.

Views of the Park from the House

The plants and the fresh air of the garden literally embrace the house. It is, in fact, the large open views of the garden that constitute one of the most pleasant and special aspects of Villar Perosa. Life in the open, especially during the summer, is indeed the most important characteristic of the villa.

Large bouquets of flowers such as fuchsias and geraniums decorate the rooms of the house and the verandas in summer.

The healthy and beckoning meadows, with their gentle vista, which is rare indeed in Italy, frames Villar Perosa in a wash of green.

The streets and squares of Villar are covered with a carpet of gravel consisting of straw-colored pebbles from the Po River. Every morning, residents awaken to the reassuring sound of the rake on the gravel together with the lively sound of birds in the garden.

A geranium (Pelargonium) *border on the east side of the house.*

Above: Details of jonquil and the camellia blossoms.

Opposite: The 'Mephisto' rose.

The circular fountain in front of the main facade.

Preceding spread: A pyramid-shaped yew, Taxus baccata, *and beech wood,* Fagus sylvatica.

Snow covers the garden on the east side of the house.

Views of the immediate garden from the house.

Bibliography

AA. VV. Extracts of *La Donna.* Turin: 1908–17.

AA. VV. Extracts of *L'Eco del Chisone.* Pinerolo: 1906–14.

AA. VV. Extracts of *La Nuova stampa.* 1935, 1945.

AA. VV. Extracts of *La Stampa.* 1935–55.

AA. VV. *Il Piemonte dei grandi viaggiatori.* Rome: Abete, 1991.

AA. VV. *San Germano, Chisone, Pramollo, Villar Perosa. . . .* Pinerolo: Tipografia Sociale, 1992.

Agnelli, Marella. Article in *Connaissance des Arts.* Paris: June 1962.

———. Article in *Gardenia.* Giorgio Mondadori Editore, May 1984.

———, and Luca Pietromarchi. *Gardens of the Italian Villas.* New York: Rizzoli, 1987.

Agnelli, Susanna. *Vestivamo alla marinara.* Milan: Arnoldo Mondadori Editore, 1986.

Beattie, William. *The Waldenses or Protestant Valleys of Piedmont, Dauphiny and the Ban de la Roche.* London: 1836.

Bernardi, M. *I cinquant'anni della R.I.V.* Turin: R.I.V., 1956.

Biscaretti di Ruffia, Carlo. *Dattiloscritto del centro storico Fiat.* 30 July 1955.

Black, Jeremy. "The Grand Tour and Savoy-Piedmont in the Eighteenth Century." *Studi piemontesi* 12, no. 2.

Carutti, Domenico. *Città di Pinerolo.* Pinerolo: Chiantore, 1893.

———. *Storia di Vittorio Amadeo II.* Turin: Carlo Clausen, 1897.

Casalis, Goffredo. *Dizionario geografico degli Stati di S.M. il Re di Sardegna.* Vol. 25. Turin: 1854.

Castronovo, Valerio. *Giovanni Agnelli: La Fiat dal 1899 al 1945.* Turin: Einaudi, 1977.

Cazzullo, Aldo. *I Ragazzi di via Po.* Milan: Arnoldo Mondadori Editore, 1997.

Chevalley, G. *Gli architetti, l'architettura e la decorazione delle ville piemontesi del XVIII secolo.* Turin: S.T.E.N., 1912.

Cicala, Vittorio. *Ville e castelli d'Italia.* Milan: Berardi, 1911.

Come vivevano, Pinerolo, Val Chisone e Germinasca fin de siècle (1880–1920), a cura di Carlo Papini.

De Amices, Edmondo. *Alle porte d'Italia.* Rome: 1884.

DeMatteis, Giuseppe. *L'eredità storica nella formazione della regione.* Turin: Università degli Studi, 1970.

Enciclopedia dei Comuni d'Italia, Il Piemonte paese per paese. Florence: Bonechi, 1995.

Friedman, Alan. *Fiat and the Network of Italian Power.* New York: NAL Books, 1989.

Gabrielli, Giuseppe. *Una vita per l'aviazione.* Milan: Bompiani, 1982.

Galli, Giancarlo. *Gli Agnelli.* Milan: Arnoldo Mondadori Editore, 1997.

Godino, Eugenio. "Villar Perosa" in "San Germano, Villar Pinasca, Pramollo etc." In *Pinerolo e il Pinerolese.* Pinerolo: 1922.

Grappini, F. *Gente di nostra stirpe.* Vol. 1. Turin: Mantovani, 1930.

Griseri, Angela. "Documenti per l'esotismo nella decorazione in Piemonte." *Studi piemontesi* 14, no. 2.

Gritella, Gianfranco. *Juvarra, l'architettura.* Vol. 2. Modena: Franco Cosimo Panini.

Grossi, Amadeo. *Coreografia della città e provincia di Pinerolo.* Turin: Stamperia Pane e Barberis, 1800.

Manno, Antonio. *Il patriziato subalpino.* Bologna: Forni Editore, 1872.

Mola Di Noaglio, Gustavo. *Genealogy and History of the Agnelli Family.* Unpublished manuscript.

Nicholson, Nigel. *Great Houses.* 1968.

19th Century European Paintings, Drawings and Watercolours. Catalogue. London: Sotheby's, 19 November 1997.

Ojetti, Ugo. *Lettere alla moglie, 1915–1919, a cura di F. Ojetti.* Florence: 1964.

Ouspensky, P. D. *In Search of the Miraculous: Fragments of an Unknown Teaching.* New York: Harcourt Brace and World, 1949.

Page, Russell. *The Education of a Gardener.* London and Glasgow: Collins, 1962.

———. "House and Garden." In *20th-Century Decorating, Architecture, and Gardens.* Edited by Mary Jane Pool. London: Weidenfeld and Nicolson, 1980.

Paroletti, Modesto. *Viaggio romantico pittorico delle provincie occidentali dell'antica e moderna Italia.* Vol. 1. Turin: Stamperie Felice Festa.

Pascal, A. *I valdesi di Val Perosa.* Torre Pellice: Soc. Studi Valdesi, 1957.

Pedrini, Augusto. *Ville dei secoli XVII e XVIII in Piemonte.* Turin: Rotocalco Dagnino, 1965.

Pietra, Italo. *I tre Agnelli.* Milan: Garzanti, 1985.

Pittavnio, Arnaldo. *Storia di Pinerolo e del Pinerolese.* Milan: Bramante Editrice, 1963.

Rovere, Clemente. *Il Piemonte antico e moderno delineato e descritto da Clemente Rovere.* Vol. 1. Rome: Soc. Reale Mutua Assicurazioni, 1978.

Sainte Croix. *Relazione del Piemonte del segretario francese Sainte Croix.* Stamperia Reale di Torino, 1876.

Strafforello, Gustavo. *La Patria geografica dell'Italia.* Vol. 2, *Provincia di Torino.* Rome, Turin, Naples: 1890.

Timbaldi, Luigi. *Uomini e montagne pinerolesi.* Pinerolo: Scuola tipografica padri Pellegrini, 1957.

Van Zuylen, Gabrielle, and Marina Schinz. *The Gardens of Russell Page.* New York: Stewart, Tabori & Chang, 1991.

Viaggiatori britannici alle valli valdesi. Edited by G. Tourn. Turin: Claudiana, 1994.

Vitullo, Fulvio. *I Marchesi Turinetti di Priero.* Turin: Tarditi, 1957.

Whitsley, Fred. Article in *Country Life,* 18 July 1985.